Travellers' Tales

from

Heaven & Hell.

Editor Dan Hiscocks

Foreword Victoria Riches
(member of the McVitie's Penguin Polar Relay -
first all womens expedition to the North Pole.)

Travellers' Tales from Heaven & Hell
2nd Edition
October 1999
published by TravellersEye Ltd.

Head Office:
Colemore Farm
Colemore Green
Bridgnorth
Shropshire
WV16 4ST
United Kingdom.
Tel: (01746) 766447
Fax: (01746) 766665
website: www.travellerseye.com
e-mail : books@travellerseye.com

First Edition published October 1997.

ISBN 0 -953 - 0575 - 18

Set in Times

All articles in Travellers' Tales from Heaven and Hell have been accepted
for publication in good faith. Readers are however advised that neither the
editor nor publisher can accept responsibility for statements made in the
articles. Furthermore the views expressed by the contributors are their
own and do not necessarily reflect that of the publisher or editor.

Reprinted and bound in Great Britain by Creative Print and Design Group

Generously sponsored by

STA TRAVEL

World leaders in young
independent travel

Preface

In some ways I always think that prefaces are a waste of time and space as very few people seem to read them. You are obviously curious, or drawn to the logos of the sponsors who kindly supported Travellerseye in this project. I would like to thank them for their support, but also for helping to grab your attention to read this.

'Travellers Tales from Heaven & Hell' is made up of the best entries in a nationwide competition we ran earlier this year. We wanted to put together a collection of short amusing tales that typically get told 'down the pub' or 'over food'. We were overwhelmed by the response and hope that the stories reflect a balance of amusing, evocative and informative tales. Reading the entries was great fun and I found myself relating to many of the emotions the experiences evoked.

It is interesting to note that the youngest contributor was ten years old (River of Life), and the oldest ninety (and wants to remain anonymous!). Another surprise was the type and location of the experience. This was often different to what I imagined the entries would be. I am pleased to say that this is now to become an annual competition and if you are interested in finding out more, please send a SAE to Travellerseye for details.

We often feel isolated with our feelings as we can't perceive that anyone else could begin to imagine how strong they can be. No matter who we are, we all have ups and downs, and whilst the causes of these are individual, the emotion isn't. A hellish day for me may be seen as a heavenly day by someone in a less fortunate position, but to me, I can only work within the emotional spectrum of my social conditioning. My interpretation of the feeling is therefore valid - as is everyones.

Recognising that others are able to relate and that we are not alone with our ups and downs helps break-down the barriers many feel important to put up. Feelings are what differentiates us from being mechanical. Society's pressures force many into an almost mechanical state. For most, life is full of 'shoulds', 'musts' and 'oughts' - and as guidelines much can be achieved with this, but we shouldn't forget that we are not machines and need to have time away from social and working pressures to take stock of what the purpose of life is.

Travel gives one this vital space.

Dan Hiscocks 1997.

Foreword

When I was asked to write a foreword for this book I was thrilled and very honoured. I also felt it was especially appropriate, having just participated in the first all women's expedition to the North Pole- the ultimate 'heavenly and hellish' experience!

This book shows that one person's idea of heaven may be another person's idea of hell. Most people think that I must have been to hell and back while walking to the North Pole, but it was in fact the most heavenly experience of my life. Many people sent in entries about their hellish journeys, but remarkably similar ones were sent in as heavenly experiences!

The time spent reading all the entries gave me a chance to explore the opportunities that travel offers. Not just the obvious ones i.e. the discovery of the country and its people, but the fact that everyone's life is altered by each journey - however small or insignificant. People come back having reassessed and re-evaluated what is important to them. It is often difficult for families and friends to comprehend this change since they have not lived through the same experiences. We must never judge another by their perception of an experience. We all see things differently; wouldn't life be boring if we all saw things the same?

As a member of the first all women expedition to the North Pole, I have seen first hand how the same experience has effected us all in different ways. Some have outwardly remained unchanged - same job, same life, but inwardly they have re-evaluated their outlook on life. Others have changed more overtly. I for one have given up a successful career in recruitment to return to college and re train as a primary school teacher. Why are we all so different? There is no answer. If I recount a little of our expedition, you, the readers, will each perceive it as either absolute heaven or total hell.

Imagine the following.... You have just spent two years, mentally and physically preparing for the adventure of a lifetime. You have never been to the arctic and the nearest you have got to proper deep snow is attempting a 'red run' on a ski slope, while slightly hung over.

We were all taken up to Resolute Bay, a remote arctic 'town' where we completed three weeks of vigorous training. How to become an arctic expert over night! However, before you know what is happening, you are on a tiny planer flying low over the stunning mountain range that makes up Ellesmere Island. You are flying direct into the mid night sun and are heading for a place where very few men and no women have ever walked before. The plane suddenly starts to bank and coming through the clouds you see a vast expanse of whiteness that is to be 'home' for the next three weeks. The approach to the 'run way' starts. A runway is half a mile by quarter of a mile of 'flat' ice. The plane prepares to land, we brace ourselves, but the wheels touch and then it takes off again. Our hearts sink, what is wrong we ask ourselves. We are now twelve hours from Resolute Bay so surely we won't have to turn back. The pilot tells us that he has to check that the ice can hold the weight of the plane - so he will touch down a few times before actually landing. Great comfort!! Four nervous 'explorers' are now terrified. What on earth are we doing here? our stomachs are somewhere near our feet, and my eyes are certainly moist with tears and fear.

After an eternity, probably half an hour, the plane finally lands. Considering the plane is landing on hard packed ice and snow, the pilot manages an incredibly comfortable landing. We only bump off our seats a couple of times. An hour later, having unloaded all our gear and had a brief catch up with the previous team, we are ready to set off. The plane's door closes and the engines start, it disappears into the distance and we are alone, fifteen hours away from the nearest help. I do not know what to feel, a range of emotions go through my mind.... I want to go home. I am so lucky to be here. I am so proud to be British. What am I doing? I can't give up because all my friends, family and the press will think I'm a wimp. Help!! No time to think, we had to start to walk before frost bite sets in. We set off for three weeks of just heading North.

However it is not 'just heading North'. This place which I am so lucky to be in, is without a doubt the most beautiful place on earth. Imagine a landscape with every shade of blue, white and black. The scenery changes every day, literally as the ice moves apart and crunches together. The arctic must be the noisiest place on earth. the ice makes a rumbling noise - like a tube train coming out of the tunnel - as it crashes together and the snow / ice crunching under your feet sounds like the first bite of an apple or the sound of an aeroplane coming out of the clouds. the ice formations would be a geologists dream. Every type of stalagmite and stalactite imaginable, and in all this beautiful shade of electric blue. Thousands of massive ice chunks that have just been thrown in the air and left as they landed, all higgledy piggledy, but still in some kind of arctic order. The whole scene is just impossible to describe without doing it injustice.

Just imagine this and maybe it helps to explain why we all see things differently, and what I imagine to be hell is your heaven and vice-versa. Happy Reading.

Victoria Riches 1997.

Acknowledgements

We are enormously grateful for everyone who took the time to enter the competition and we are only sorry that more of the entries weren't able to be included in the final book. A large reason for the enormous response must be put down to the publicity the competition received. We would like to thank the following publications for their generous support.

Spirit, Maxim, The Great Outdoors, Geographical Magazine, Traveller, Independent on Sunday, Sunday Telegraph, Writers News, Writers Monthly.

We must also thank all the artists who visualised the essence of the tales. Many thanks to:

David Armstrong, Gabriel Bristow, Amy Cooper, William Cooper, Joel Carter, Tom Dawes, Alec Dawes, Daniel Gough, William Greenshield, Sam Hiscocks, Oliver Hiscocks, Oliver Howell, Laura Hollingsworth, William Morely, Thomas Pollard, William Pollard, Robert Sellwood, Gemma Sheldon Brown, Emily Taylor, Ben Taylor, Gemma Watson.

We would also like to thank the judges:- Jennifer Cox from Lonely Planet, Simon Calder from The Independent, and Gillian Smith from STA Travel:

Many have given their time and support which has been invaluable, in particular Claire Gough, Matt Barker, Mark Edgington, Ruth Ruckley and Jill Ibberson.

This book is dedicated to my mother.
A BIG thank you to you all.

Contents

A FAIR EXCHANGE.

The regal-looking hand beckoned me. His little finger nail almost two inches long - a status symbol, demonstrating that such a man does not stoop to manual work. He was a money changer.

This was Kano - an ancient and proud trading city in northern Nigeria - a major cross-roads of Trans Saharan trade. I sat in the shade of the old slave house, amidst the chaotic Kurmi Market.

Yusef, a Hausa man, and his fellow money changers, operated parallel to the banks. With an exchange rate substantially better than banks, they are into a thriving business. It's illegal of course - but his ancestors were here centuries before the banks. They are in great demand by traders from neighbouring Chad, Cameroon or Niger.

Yusef rubbed his hands together at the thought of business. "You are welcome ... sit down."

Laid out in front of him were pieces of local jewellery, providing cover for his illicit trade, in case an inquisitive policeman wandered past.

"Do you want pounds or dollars?"

"Pounds" I said, staring into his eyes. He gave nothing away, no hint of being desperate, nor of being flushed with foreign currency.

Business was not to be hurried and I was served with hot, sweet tea. I wafted away the flies that buzzed incessantly around my head.

Yusef said nothing, just noisily slurping tea from his glass, and staring at me through dull eyes. He was trying to weigh me up before the real negotiations began.

I copied him, sipping my tea - waiting. His black, doleful face studied me intently. Tribal scars etched high on his cheeks added to his sadness. Yusef slurped his tea again, he was in no hurry.

Negotiations began after the third glass.

"...Now," he said warmly, rubbing his hands again, "How much do you want to change?"

"That...," I said, in as slow and cool a voice I could muster - "That depends on what exchange rate you are prepared to give me."

An hour of patient, intense and delicate haggling passed. But always in polite and subdued tones.

Believing the climax had been reached and praying that the time was ripe, I paused, then committed myself. "... And, that is my final offer."

Yusef stared hard, his eyebrows lifting in surprise, but he said nothing for a full minute. The tension was unbearable.

The first one to speak - loses, I thought.

The silence continued: seconds felt like hours. Thinking I had blown the whole deal I was about revise my offer. I bit my tongue and held my breath.

"You are a hard man," declared Yusef shaking his head in disbelief, he looked totally defeated.

We shook hands and he counted out a wad of local bank notes. Yusef was all smiles now, he had got exactly what he wanted ... my pounds. I wondered, in spite of his comments, just who had got the best deal - him or me? In Africa you can never tell.

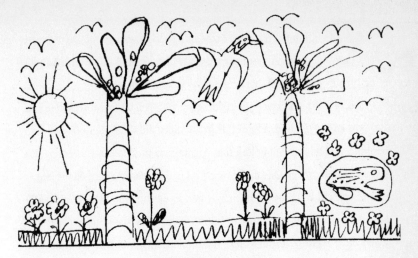

PARADISE LOST.

There's such a place as Paradise, I've been there. Twelve hours of tropical sunshine each day with a drop of rain between midnight and two in the morning every Thursday. Not that there was any way of telling Thursday from Tuesday. I was bumming around Indonesia and Paradise was a tiny tropical island called Gili Something? I was sharing a bamboo beach hut with an Australian girl called Lizzy.

There was beautiful clear blue water with coral castles and technicolour fish. They went in for stripes and trailing fins like silk scarves. I lay in the sunshine drinking coconut milk all day and killer black rice wine at night, with a party every so often and Lizzy to love me. She was as supple as a gymnast and clever with it. She was a genius below the neck was Lizzy. I don't mean that as a put down. Head cleverness messes things up half the time whether it comes from men or women, and I'm not implying that Lizzy was thick, she was just relatively free of silly ideas about men doing the cooking and washing up. She was content to do the few chores there are on a tropical island and leave me to fulfil my proper function in life which is lying in the sun. Lying in the sunshine I give off good vibes like those holy men who sit cross legged on mountains. I probably do more good for mankind lying on a tropical beach than a clutch of vicars on bicycles.

Lizzy was a good bit younger than me, but then so are most people and I'm past caring about that age stuff, it certainty didn't put her off. She was blondish and this biscuit colour that Australians used to be before they got scared of skin cancer. One of the reasons I had to work so hard on the beach was to try and catch up with Lizzy's tan. Even the bits that are normally covered by a bikini were brown. I don't know why she bothered with me when there were beautiful young Indonesian lads with hair like Shetland ponies and the bodies of limbo dancers.

They couldn't half bop, these Indonesian lads, high energy disco they did. It was like watching fifty Michael Jacksons and a dozen artists formally known as Prince. I looked like a cart horse in comparison and tended to collapse after the third dance even if I'd not been drinking rice wine.

It never gave me a hangover though so I was usually alright before Lizzy went to fetch breakfast. In the afternoon; after my swim she would read to me while I sunbathed and she was a dab hand at massaging my back and washing my hair.

I quite took to Lizzy. She never expected to be kissed or made a fuss of except during moments of passion and she never got upset when I petted the Swedes or Germans before they went off with the Indonesian lads. Our two weeks on the island cost us about ten quid each. I was on the verge of sending home for my savings and staying for a couple of years when I realised Lizzy wasn't all I'd cracked her up to be.

I should have realised something was wrong when she wore her white tennis skirt and high-heeled sandals to bring my breakfast one morning. Normally she just wore a sarong or a Swan Lager T-shirt. She'd got hold of half a bottle of whisky from somewhere. She was dead resourceful, Lizzy, it comes of having convicts for ancestors. She gave me a massage before carrying my mat, pillow and suntan lotion the whole five yards to the beach. All day she was more attentive than usual and smiled so much you'd have thought she was auditioning for a Pepsodent advert.

It crossed my mind that she was going crazy.

In the evening she took me to a little restaurant and we had candles (on the table I mean, not to eat). Lizzy wore some sparkly earrings and eye make-up. Apart from a couple of denim shirts with the arms torn out I only had my sunbathing jockstrap and a sarong. The rest of my luggage had been lost in Jakarta.

They don't do expensive food on Gili Something. What we ate that night was lots of fishy dishes, coconut and cucumber salad, fruit that had been stewed in brandy for a couple of days with real cream on top.

I became nervous because Lizzy was making such a production of it all but I was gob-smacked when she told me what it was all about.

"Do you know what day it is?"

"Er.....is it Tuesday?"

Lizzy sighed again.

"It's February the twenty ninth.... will you marry me?"

I left the island by the first boat in the morning. I think something similar happened to Adam in the Bible.

BIG MAMA MAFIA.

It is truly extraordinary how the events of travel change. One minute a quick and painless death is the best you could wish for, next you are sitting in miraculous sunshine getting drunk with complete strangers, laughing at your inability to speak their language.

Possibly the second biggest town in Colombia is a rather unsavoury sprawling mass of concrete answering to the name of Medallin. The Triumph was sucking fumes off the reserve tank so I headed towards the seedy part of town in the hope of changing some greenbacks to buy fuel. Rounding a sharp bend, my not so good day turned into a disaster as the back tyre went down dumping me in the gutter. Lying on my back, unhurt but close to tears with frustration, the sky was working up to a drenching of monumental proportions, and it was still only 11.00 am!

"You need help?" I will never know if this was meant as a statement or a question. I scrutinised the thirty something owner of the slurred voice. He was better dressed than most in this part of town, and an expensive looking hair cut flopped from side to side as he swayed around trying not to spill a bottle of strong Colombian beer. Willy had exhausted his English vocabulary so his younger brother Eddy was dragged out of another bar to translate. In minutes my fortunes changed as it became crystal clear this family had clout.

Willy changed dollars, while a small army of ragged people pushed my bike to a closed garage where the proprietor was duly summoned to fix the tyre and fill with petrol. Willy invited me to stay and led me to a very posh fortified apartment block on the edge of town. He then introduced me to half a dozen men sitting around on big settees smoking and drinking. Each introduction started with, "..and this is my brother". The only woman was Eddy's exquisite nineteen year old wife, heavily pregnant. In total there were nine brothers but no sisters.

There was some heated conversation between Eddy and "Wayne",(closest translation), the eldest. "Now I have to talk to Mama", he explained, "She is a manic depressive and has not left her room in two years." After a few minutes Eddy emerged saying Mama wanted to see me. A grey beached whale with piercing dark eyes studied a filthy white traveller from her huge bed surrounded by plates of half-eaten food. The frilly nightdress beckoned me forward for a closer look. Plump fingers prodded and grabbed at my non existent biceps. "Mama says you have no strength to do this thing so you must have courage - you are family and Wayne is to look after you in our town". In seconds I was sitting in the best chair drinking deliciously cold beer. Wayne fixed me with his mother's unyielding dark eyes demanding "mokie mokie". Experience of travelling in countries where my single linguistic skill is asking for a beer, I resort to the slow nod and gentle smile when faced with an armed stranger aggressively making noises. In this case it paid off and I was handed a cigarette.

Two or three puffs later several people were dragging me off the ceiling.

Such is the effect of hallucinogenic drugs, but the overall effect was rather astounding, and my Spanish, or at least some language that I did not understand but clearly everybody else did, flowed from my tongue.

One loses track of time in such a state, but after an hour or a week, Eddy suggested we go for a walk. He, plus spouse, and I squeezed into the back of a minute taxi with no rear seat, while Wayne sat in the front, polishing his handgun. After a short but uncomfortable journey we arrived at the foot of a heavily wooded mountain and proceeded to climb. Wayne kept up a constant impassioned banter. I was convinced he was just telling me the manner he planned to dispose of my body and frankly I was in no condition to care. I was relieved when the summit revealed a broad flat plateau fringed with stout trees (each harbouring a flock of pink flying elephants!) Pungent food stalls billowed smoke into the early evening sky as we fought through the crowd. Like a fool, I wandered off and in a few yards was completely lost. There I stood, drugged to the eyeballs, with no idea where my hosts lived, where my bike was, and couldn't even guess at their family name.

Eventually, Eddy with Wayne on his shoulders forced their way through the throng. I expected to be summarily executed, but Wayne was relieved to see me as Mama would not have approved of him losing her new family member.

Brilliant sunshine invaded my room at daybreak, and the aroma of fresh Colombian coffee had me searching for the kitchen. Three walls were clad in matching rococo cupboards, with the fourth revealing the source of this family's wealth. Vast glass jars were stacked to the ceiling crammed full of newly harvested marijuana. My new found friends were simple farmers earning a living like any other.

That evening was spent in the bosom of this welcoming family, laughing and drinking. It was time for me to head off once more on the Pan

American Highway towards Ecuador. Before my departure, Wayne gave me a straw hat to keep the sun off, Eddy a lock knife with a four inch blade to keep me safe, and Willy a bag of marijuana the size of a Coke can to keep me happy. These things in their opinion were all I needed for a successful journey! Mama gave me a sloppy kiss and her blessing. This was probably the best gift of all. Reflecting back on my ridiculous adventure, the days in Medallin will always be one of the highlights because of the genuine good natured people it was my privilege to meet.

SWAMI BILL AND THE SHARK PIT.

Swami Bill was a yoga teacher who had taken far too many drugs in his life. He and I worked in a youth camp on the island of Eleuthera, Bahamas in the summer of 1985. One afternoon we hitched a ride to the old chicken factory by a bay, where the entrails that used to be thrown off the cliff had attracted a number of sharks. We had heard that they still came back, and so armed with the inside of our frozen chicken and some hooks we launched the line. We used the plastic bag (previously carrying our giblets) as a float and watched it bob like a man o'war. Nothing happened.

Suddenly there was a flash. A glimpse of white around impenetrable black, and the float disappeared..

"SHIT" shouted Swami Bill, "FUCK MAN, FUCK". The coils whipped out to sea. Bill started running after them.

"Don't run that way, run the other way," I called.

"I'm not running, I'M BEING PULLED."

I grabbed the waistband of Bill's shorts and leant back. We ran forward together.

"Shit, that's fucking killing me man, hold somewhere else." I let go and to stop Bill getting away I threw my arms around his neck, toppling him. The line went taught - singing.

"Bill, I think..." The line moved. "I don't believe this. I do not fucking believe this." Incredibly, the line actually began to drag the two of us slowly along the ground. I suddenly got scared.

"Let go of the line. Let go of the fucking line!" Ahead I could see the cliff edge marking the drop to the pit below. "LET IT GO BILL!"

"I CAN'T."

Ross Camidge

"What do you mean you can't?" The rocky surface was skinning us in places.

"I tied it around my wrist. Ow Shit!"

"Well I'm going to let you die you motherfucker unless you get it off your wrist right now."

"I can't man I can't. I think I'm going to lose my hand!"

"You're going to lose more than that if we go over that cliff to the fucking shark!"

"Don't leave me man, don't leave me. Tell me you won't leave me."

I'm not proud of it, but I was ready to bail out. That awful moment when you have to face the music and you realise that in all your fantasies you're a hero and in real life you're just as scared as everyone else.

"Bill man, I can't hold on. I just can't..."

"DON'T YOU FUCKING LEAVE ME!"

I began to relax my grip on his shoulders. "Bill, I..."

The line broke.

We were maybe three feet from the edge. I got up straight away, dusting myself off, but Bill lay on the ground for a minute or two. I found a knife. He cut the line from his wrist. It was bloody in places.

AN ADVENTUROUS DINNER.

A casual passer-by could easily miss Bentley's restaurant in Quito (Ecuador). The only clue is a discreetly placed menu beside the wrought iron gates screening an attractive colonial style house. But that menu is mouth-watering.

A sign on the front door said OPEN so we rang the bell. The small elegantly furnished dining room into which we were shown had an atmosphere more of a private house than a restaurant: thick carpet, well polished antique furniture, old prints on the walls. There are several different sized rooms, but as it was a quiet evening, one of the smaller ones was being used.

Owner Ron Coffey welcomed us and discussed our orders - some dishes are specialities which he, his wife and their chef have spent years perfecting. All are very reasonably priced and portions are ample. Candles were lit, drinks served and the scene seemed set for a luxurious and relaxed evening, just the sort of pampering appreciated after five strenuous weeks travelling around South America.

Little did I know that my adventures were not yet over. When Mr Coffey nonchalantly told us not to be alarmed if a tiger appeared we all laughed. Surely he had to be joking? Not so.

We were part way through the main course when in stalked Sasha, a three foot high sixty pound fully-grown Margay tiger. He leapt straight onto one astonished gentleman's lap. Once we had recovered from the initial surprise Sasha became the focus of attention and topic of conversation. As we admired his sleek coat and huge luminous eyes he prowled restlessly around, pausing now and then to appraise one of the diners. No-one was prepared for what happened next.

I felt a thump and a searing pain in my upper arm. "He's bitten me," I screamed. Cutlery clattered to plates. All eyes turned in my direction. Amid horror and consternation Sasha was hustled from the room.

Deranged by shock and frantic to discover the extent of the damage but frustrated by the tight long sleeve of my dress, I asked Sylvia to unzip the back and pull it off my shoulder. Equally deranged, she began to comply. This spontaneous strip act was only halted by a suggestion that we go somewhere more private.

A couple of claw marks and a large bruise on my right arm, with a tear in the sleeve of a favourite dress, were to provide subsequent proof that I had neither dreamed nor invented the incident. After all, how often do you go out for a quiet dinner and end up being attacked by a tiger .... and live to tell the tale?

The attack happened so quickly it was difficult to piece together what took place and why. One theory is that Sasha was simply trying to attract my attention - he had not bitten, but clawed, my arm. Another is that he was unsettled by my Indian-made fabric bag which I had placed underneath my chair - when he was grabbed away from me he picked up this bag in his mouth. One thing is certain: Sasha had never before attacked a guest. So I made history.

Still traumatised, we nevertheless managed to enjoy the rest of the excellent meal. An offer of complimentary liqueurs was accepted and, after the largest Drambuie I have ever drunk, Sasha sat placidly on my lap like an outsize cat.

Ron Coffey, an Irish-American, had bought Sasha six years previously as a five day old cub whose mother had been shot; he was not expected to live. But Coffey was experienced in handling animals to re-introduce to the wild. Within twenty four hours American Airlines responded to his request to fly in supplies of a special blend of dehydrated milk prescribed by New York Zoological Society.

For three months Coffey and his Ecuadorian wife, Bruma, devotedly bottle-fed that tiger cub every hour (day and night), gradually extending the interval over the next two months. Sasha now eats three pounds of cooked meat a day, likes three egg yolks for breakfast and drinks low-fat milk.

Because he has never been permitted to eat anything raw he cannot be returned to the wild, but he has never been penned and is accustomed to having the freedom of both house and restaurant. He sleeps (under an electric blanket) by day and is always fed and exercised before being allowed into the restaurant area in the evening. So he is normally perfectly safe, but nevertheless makes an excellent security guard, as a couple of prospective burglars discovered one night when he defended his territory.

If you are ever in Quito a visit to Bentley's* is highly recommended.

Food, decor and service are impeccable and the floor show unforgettable - where else in the world would a tiger join you for dinner? Give my regards to Sasha.

*Bentley's is at Juan Leon Mera 404, just behind the Avenida Amazonas at the Hotel Colon end of the road.

SAD BUT TRUE.

As I was going through the inner door of one of the many ladies' toilets at Heathrow Airport, an old lady on crutches was struggling to come out. Obligingly I held the door open for her and her crutches. I then thought I would do the real Good Samaritan bit and went to the outer door and opened that for her - but as she passed through I let go of the door and accidentally elbowed her on the shoulder, knocking her to the ground. As I struggled to help her up, someone came barging through the door, knocking me down on top of her!

Although the old lady assured me, after I had picked her up, that she was "all right", I never quite believed her. To this day I still have nightmares about it!

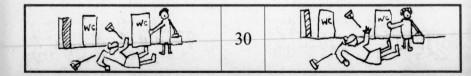

WORM HOLE.

The middle of Africa in the middle of Spring. I'd been swimming in the source of the Nile and all was well...and then I started getting these marks all over my body. Being in the heart of Africa, free from the glare of perfect skin advertisements, I shrugged off the marks as some irritation or other.

Things progressed. The marks became lumps and it was time to consult my 'do-it-yourself health assessment guide for idiots in the jungle'. Within ten minutes I'd found the problem and the solution: 'Boils and Hot Compresses', page three. I didn't read much further because the book got quite gruesome after that and the sun was shining outside. It always did.

So it was that every night that week I would heat water and press hot flannels onto the lumps, patiently waiting for the boils to form heads whence they could be lanced. It wasn't happening. They were rapidly becoming the size of golf balls. However, confident with my blissfully undramatic diagnosis, I soldiered on in the role of Brit abroad; red and blotchy.

Then it happened; pain and suffering. My right arm overnight had swollen to the size and shape of a rugby ball. The boil that had sat so elegantly on my wrist had now been enveloped with puffy flesh. A small hole remained into which I could peer observing a pulsating motion. White fluid rising to the surface of the skin and then descending once more to the hidden depths, where my wrist used to be. This was unpleasant and was not described on page four of my idiot's guide, or anywhere else in the first chapter. This was the stuff of volume two, which I hadn't been able to fit into my rucksack.

The hospital did not inspire confidence. The walls weren't painted white for a start, a prerequisite in my mind to the word "hospital". In fact nothing in my experience had prepared me for this. I couldn't equate anything I saw with anything I'd learnt to entrust my health to. Thankfully I was wrong. A doctor approached me. He was a small man wearing ripped trousers which were covered in the red muddy soil that was everywhere, a blood stained handkerchief was knotted around an injured finger. He did not acknowledge me but grabbed my wrist, squeezed it slightly, mumbled something to the nurse and then disappeared. The nurse asked me to follow her.

"What did he say, what's wrong?"

A failed attempt to sound calm. The nurse grinned and informed the missionary translator who was with me of my condition. The missionary woman, a very attractive blond American smiled at me, "maggots" she said, and walked off after the nurse. I was left on the wooden seat weakly lodging my complaint;

"but its boils. I read it. I've got boils."

I followed down corridors lined with what seemed like hundreds of

African mothers standing with their babies, every kid screaming, every mother jogging their child up and down rhythmically, calmly. I was not calm. Into the hospital's operating theatre I did go.

The same doctor stood with his back to me, drawing up a syringe. Gauzes and bandages strewn about the floor. I am directed to undress. This I do and find myself sat on the theatre table in my underpants, bulging with boils, in the presence not only of the missionary, two nurses and the doctor, but also before an audience of grinning kids. The room had a window looking out onto a large area of wasteland. A leaping gang of children had gathered and were screaming with laughter at "mazungoo" in the nude. I grinned back weakly.

The doctor began to squeeze my wrist whilst I continued to argue my case for boils and that the doctor should not squeeze "until the hot compresses have formed heads on the red lumps"... when out pops a two centimetre maggot from the hole in my wrist. The maggot lands on my thigh and begins crawling towards my knee. The doctor flicks the maggot onto the floor and stands on it. The children cheer. Missionary and nurses squeal with delight. I feel rather strange.

The job was finished by the two nurses and the missionary, who seemed to take an inordinate amount of pleasure removing the maggots from my back and shoulders, chatting and laughing away as if they were picking strawberries.

I left the hospital slightly sore, slightly elated, and clutching a milk bottle containing white fluid. This was to be rubbed on my body twice a day. It stank.

The next day the missionary came running up to where I was staying, breathlessly apologising and explaining that the white fluid had to be diluted

1:10. I'd already used the stuff three times and my skin was peeling rapidly. I poured the fluid into a saucer and left it outside hoping the lions would drink it, and then sat down to a bonfire containing one 'Idiots Guide To Health Assessment'.

RETURN TO GARABALDI.

In some of the more remote areas of the world, the easiest way in is by helicopter; but sixty years ago they did not exist, so to reach one such mountain wilderness, I had to climb.

Now I was returning to this beautiful area, recollecting what had happened sixty years before.

Our stay was coming to an end and I had climbed to great heights and had collected a rucksack full of plants.

On my way back, I came across a five hundred foot almost perpendicular wall of ice. It was getting late and would take me too long to circumnavigate, so it meant cutting steps across with my ice axe. When I got to the middle, one of the steps gave way - and down I went!

Luckily, I was able to use my ice axe as a brake, jamming it into the ice wall behind me to lessen the speed of my descent. At the bottom, I bounced onto a pile of rocks. When I came to, I was blind from the shock.

My companion was on the adjoining mountain and he fortunately saw me fall. When he reached me he picked me up and carried me back to camp. Miraculously, two nurses had just arrived and were camping nearby; they patched up my cuts and broken thumb and, in the absence of a hot water bottle, they bedded me down on the rocks heated by the camp fire. My sight returned the next day and I had recovered sufficiently in another twenty four hours to travel back.

Now this second visit was coming to an end and, reluctantly, we had to descend to civilisation. In the evening, looking up from the lodge in the valley below, we watched the sky darken and fork-lightning striking the trees in the park. Many fires sprang up and in the morning carrier-planes were still dousing the flames.

The previous trip had ended in an accident; if we had been caught up there in the storm and the forest fires this time, there could have been another one. As it was, I was taking back memories of a wonderful adventure.

Garibaldi Provincial Park is my idea of heaven

FIVE GO MAD IN PAIGNTON.

Going on holiday with the family probably ranks alongside taking exams, moving house, getting married and giving birth, as one of the most stressful things you can do. Last year my mum and dad asked me if I would like to go on holiday with them (granddad and the dog) to a small seaside resort for a week or so, and as my imaginary tall handsome Italian boyfriend had not yet materialised to whisk me off to the Bahamas, I agreed. I don' t know whether we are unique or not, but going on holiday for the Dixons basically means trying to recreate your home in a different environment. We went to 'The Look Out' Hotel, Paignton. It soon became clear that this title was a warning and not just a comment on the sea view. Well, certainly mum and dad had a pleasant enough view. From my bedroom window (round the back of the hotel) I had a lovely view of the 9.15 leaving Paignton's railway station. (This must be what they referred to as 'easy access' in the travel brochure).

It's hard to describe the owner of our hotel, 'Uncle Tom'. Yet despite the fact that I am a grown woman, he's Irish and I'm English, and I'd never seen him before in my life, this man insisted on becoming my Uncle. He's certainly not like any Uncle I've ever had but I guess he's strange enough to qualify as a relation of ours. He's Irish - not just 'of Ireland' but that rare species that all stereotypes are built on. Yes, he even says 'Jay-sus', and has that knack of repeating everything he says immediately after he's said it. One shining example of his initiative as a hotel-owner is the marvellous idea of having soft toys on your dining table. I guess it could be down to the 'Uncle' syndrome again, the feeling you have when you receive that cute bunny napkin holder for your fifteenth birthday. There's something a little bit mysterious about them though. Like where the hell did they come from? Perhaps they are the forgotten treasures of other 'guests' who tried to make a break for it on the 11.25 from their bedroom window? The function of these delightful items is to enable Tom to illustrate visually what is on the menu for that evening's meal. Picking up a toy cow and mooing, he will shout 'lovely bit o' beef later', whilst granddad will squint at the object and enquire loudly 'what' s that he's got there then? A duck?'

Next to our dining table sits 'Big Mick' (as we all affectionately must call him), who looks like he's sat in the same chair soaking up the same banter all his life. Big Mick's side-burns nearly consume half his face. Perhaps he's soaked up so much he's beginning to turn into a soft toy himself. Big Mick and his wife come every year. They were here when Tom was in the paper for saving a diver who was trapped by the rocks. (Framed newspaper cuttings of this momentous event are proudly displayed amongst the other 'objects d'art' such as dried fish, plastic parrots and a 'Happy Holidays' plate from Majorca). Last year, Big Mick and his wife got T-shirts printed saying 'I survived the Look-Out Hotel' and wore them proudly on their final day.

Still, dealing with Uncle Tom is only half the holiday fun. Breakfast starts with a few of granddad's booming key phrases such as 'Did you sleep well?' and 'I suppose they call this a traditional breakfast', then a summary of the weather forecast. Following this, Uncle Tom arrives with his breakfast serenade of 'It's very hot, it's very hot' ('Christ, that's hot' on good days) Maximum fun is the way granddad attempts a rapport with Uncle Tom by shouting at him loudly in a broad Irish twang 'Top o' the mornin' to ya Paddy!' whilst I place my head neatly into my bowl of Cornflakes and attempt to inhale.

One day at the dinner table the background music took on a whole new dimension. Previously we had the pleasure of Paignton Amateur Operatic

Society's version of South Pacific, which was being broadcast on Paignton local radio. Depending on how quickly you finish your meal (which depends on how fast Uncle Tom snatches your plate away in preparation for the next steaming part of your meal - 'It's hot - It's hot - Jay-sus that's hot') you may or may not reach Paignton radio's discussion hour. This helped to increase my appetite no end, but no matter how fast I tried to bolt my food, we always managed to catch 'the feature'. On this occasion, the feature was a heated debate on contraception. The effectiveness of condoms, and their relevance in preventing the spread of Aids. What amazed me was the apparent acceptance of this aural wallpaper as if a pleasant melody was floating along to accompany our meal and aid its digestion. Well, acceptance by all, except dad, who gagged on his piece of beef and turned a lighter shade of puce.

Later that evening dad and I were sitting on the balcony, when a leather-skinned OAP trundled past in his trunks. Dad, whose legs are whiter than Father Christmas's beard, turned to me and said 'Why do people go in for this browning?' Something told me that there was no point in trying to explain the concepts of image and beauty to a man who wears a Marlborough suncap to protect his bald spot from burning, so I told him it was to prevent rickets and he seemed satisfied enough.

After the light fitting dripped on me, Mum said 'Would you like to come again?' Dad said 'Where else could you find a place where you can shower in the lounge and train spot from your bedroom window?' Strangely enough, my tall, handsome Italian lover has still not yet materialised, but this year alternative applications will be considered.

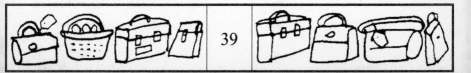

A TURKISH DELIGHT.

Sitting in a car next to an attractive Turkish man I had only met that day, (in a leather shop of course!) it seemed a night like any other night .

We arrived at the top of a hill, at a tiny outdoor taverna overlooking a valley of twinkling lights. Magic! There was no-one else but us. Snap! He clicked his fingers and beautiful music surrounded me. Snap! An earthen-ware jug of red wine was brought to our table and poured for me. Snap! A candle was placed in front of me and lit. I thought, "This man knows about women!" Exquisite morsels of local cuisine followed, with freshly-baked bread. Snap! We were alone. He gazed into my eyes and in a husky voice, entranced me through the meal with tales of his childhood and culture. Then we had thick black coffee with delicious gooey sweets and he said, "Tell me about your country." I made him laugh with tales of my life and land. A warm breeze played around my hair, he held my hand over the table and I felt beautiful.

I thought that was it, and the evening couldn't have been better, but we then drove twenty kilometres through the night to Kusdasi, to a little restaurant, to see my first belly-dancer. She wriggled a finger and twenty male diners scurried to clear their table. One man lay on it and she danced over him, extracting agonised gasps from the audience by grinding her stiletto into his groin while tauntingly swinging her tasselled and brimming lime green bikini top. Everyone's eyes were out on stalks. Wow!

No sooner had she finished, than a pyramid-shaped vision arrived at the table - three tiers of trays balanced on tiny glasses, rimmed with candles and slices of apple and dates, oranges, plump grapes and cheese. I laughed in sheer delight - it was magnificent! He said "I really love your eyes. Your eyes talk to me." I took lots of small sips of a liqueur while regaining my breath.

Unbelievably, one more surprise was in store for me, when I was already feeling flushed, radiant and like some exotic princess. (Well, blue eyes, British and blonde hair is exotic in Turkey!) I was also thinking I had never met a more romantic, thoughtful, attractive and attentive man. We walked across the street and into a large, bright, empty ballroom. It seemed the night-club had been opened just for him. He spoke quickly and authoritatively and handed something to a young man, who appeared briefly from behind the scenes. It was exciting to hear him speak and not to know what was to happen. We were plunged into darkness. Then the lights came up on a huge mirror globe above our heads which shot rainbow colours around the room. A song came on - slow and sensuous - he gently gathered me to him and we danced. Time and the world ceased to exist as we swirled in eddies of music.

I floated back to his car and he drove me back to my hotel. From the back of the car, he handed me a red rose (Allah only knows where that came from), looked deeply into my eyes (which made me quiver) and said, "Thank you for spending this memorable evening with me. You made it so special"

I will never forget that night and the memory of the spell of romance that was woven around me. We never saw one another again.

VARANISI DAWN.

This was Varanasi, one of India's holy cities, it's a place of pilgrimage for Hindus and the best place to die if you want to attain Nirvana. Sadhus clambered around the steps, cleansing themselves in the holy waters of the Ganges. We were told that many wealthy people give up their possessions and walk to Varanasi to await death. A long walk and a long wait for some who may slowly starve to death.

Breathing in the heavy smells of the river and its congregation, we were amazed people didn't die sooner. Our guide told us that non Hindus would become ill if they immersed themselves in the Ganges, and the way the boat was rocking on the current this was a possibility! Hindus apparently won't die from drinking its holy waters, but we also heard that gastro-enteritis was at epidemic proportions.

Our ageing boatman struggled to push the boat out against the swirling current around the ghats to the centre of the river. We joined crowds of other boats moored slightly up stream in the centre of the Ganges. The sun was just beginning to rise over the horizon; small boys leapt enthusiastically from lamp posts and splashed into the water, having the time of their lives. All life was here at this moment of dawn on the Ganges. People prayed and their voices were carried away in the breeze.

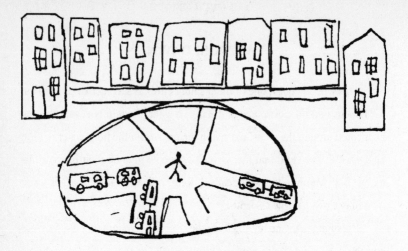

NIET WAY OUT.

What's your worst nightmare? Is it to be trapped deep underground in a strange foreign place with no means of escape, lost without trace forever? Well this nightmare became my reality when on a recent visit to Moscow. I was using their underground system; fortunately for me I "awoke" from this horror story just in the nick of time and lived to tell the tale. Others may not be quite so lucky

On the Moscow metro there are no maps, guides, or English written or spoken anywhere, just Russian characters faintly carved in stone. This is precisely why most visitors travel around the city in tourist buses. But not for me, oh no, there would be no challenge in that. If you do decide to travel on the world's most efficient (and cheapest) transport system, there are a few simple rules to remember. As my anxious Russian guide explained, to get from A to B you have to physically count each stop, so that you know when you have arrived at your destination. It was six from our hotel to the Kremlin, so I nodded furiously like a nut-case with a severe twitch each time the train stopped to be sure that I didn't make any miscalculations. That worked so well (apart from scaring the locals) that by day four confidence got the better of me and I decided to venture further afield and return from a different station. Before I left I had noted carefully that I had to change trains, as the red line converged into the green line northbound. What I had failed to notice however until it was too late was that the yellow, brown *and* blue lines also converged into what turned out to be a main hub station.

After what seemed like hours scurrying down a number of identical looking tunnels and wandering around in ever-decreasing circles trying to find that elusive green line, I realised that I was well and truly up the creek without a paddle, or more appropriately up the tunnel without a train. Yes, they may well have marbled floors you could eat your *blinniss* off, and chandeliers and statues adorning the ticket offices, but give me Paddington station any day; at least they provide coloured indicators to point you in the right direction. In desperation, I started approaching suitable looking Muscovites in the vain hope of someone who could speak English, but that plan of action failed miserably. In fact, curiously enough I seemed to attract an assortment of women of all ages who approached me for a chat. God knows what they were saying, it could have been anything from "I like your coat, hand it over comrade" to "Go home, capitalist floozy." To add to the mounting pressure, did I mention that this was supposed to be the last jaunt of my stay as I was due to catch a flight home in a few hours time that very afternoon? I could see the headlines now: "British girl survives nights and days in Moscow maze" or "My hell - by British mole."

I would still be probably down there now, had it not been for a vision in red from Essex with her friend whom I recognised from my hotel. By a sheer stroke of luck, I bumped into them in tunnel number three, also trying to figure out the finer points of Moscow's public transport. I threw myself at their mercy (and feet) and after a thousand thank-yous, pleaded with them to take me away from all this. They didn't know me from Adam but they soon did as I stuck closer to them than their thermal underwear. With a little ingenuity and reasoning they steered me through endless towering escalators and deep ranks of thick set locals and got us all back in one piece to the sanctuary of our hotel, just in time to catch my flight.

Apart from a few grey hairs and ageing ten years in two hours, I suppose no harm was done. I just wonder how many other tourists are down there now, lost in eternal limbo like that cult sixties television show the "Time Tunnel". Even Swampy himself would have found this a tough one to figure out.

RIDING THE DRAGON.

A hissing noise woke me in a Karen Hut deep in the hill forest. Opening my eyes I saw serpentine coils that seem to be emerging from the blanket - golden coils as thick as my arm. I had been trekking around the Golden Triangle visiting hill tribes. Until I hired a motorbike it had been a bit boring. Walking down a street in Bangkok or Chang Mai is always stimulating but, whether you are on foot or elephant a forest is much the same. North Thailand has massive hills and hair-pin bends. Fractured my skull on a motorbike years ago and hadn't touched one again until this trip. Perhaps Buddha gave me my confidence back. I visited a lot of hill villages and sampled opium.

They all do opium those hill tribes. I could never tell the difference from one tribe to the next, but the women had special costumes. The Ah-Ka wear bonnets full of metal studs and coins together with beads and things like football pads; the White Keren women have to wear something white everyday until they get married, and some Keren wear dozens of rings around their necks which get stretched like giraffes'. Not that I was interested in women at the time - I hit the villages for the culture and the Low Cow or whatever the local rice wine was called, and the opium.

I'd come easy riding into this village the night before and asked for a bite to eat and a rush mat to sleep on. I then wanted a pot of opium. I followed a skinny long-necked women to the local opium den, it was dimly lit with a smoky oil lamp and had a low roof and there were semi-naked children running around. Oily smoke clung to everything including the kids. My body hummed a tune and begun to numb and I relaxed. I fell asleep.

Woken by the hissing I thought my last moment had come. The only light came from gaps in the wooden walls and a small hole in the thatch. There was a smell of old opium and unwashed bodies. Just the sort of place my mum said I would end up in if I didn't eat my rice pudding.

Then the toddler I had been playing with the night before crawled on top of the blanket and woke his mother. The hissing had been her breathing and the golden coils her ringed neck.

There must be a moral here if I can just put my finger on it. Maybe the one my dad was always on about. Something to do with clean living.

THE UNFORGETTABLE JOURNEY.

On reaching Yukoma I learn that there is a possibility of a flota leaving for Rurrenabaque at 11.00 pm. It is now thundering and I'm wet through. If the flota doesn't get stuck (highly unlikely) then I'll get to Rurrenabaque at 2 am. I decide to accept a woman's offer to stay with her sister for the night. I naively imagine a small but comfortable warmish flat with the possibility of taking a shower. The woman flags down a boy on a motorbike who agrees to take me to the sister's house. We slip and slide through mud along tracks that barely exist, and 1 wonder for a moment if this is an elaborate plan to kidnap me?

I am met in the bucketing rain (the rainy season isn't supposed to start for months!) by a relative, and we walk for another half mile through giant puddles and mountains of mud. Gaby's home is a small adobe dwelling with a mud floor, no front door, two tiny beds and certainly no shower. I arrive dripping and mud-streaked. We sit silently in the candlelight after brief introductions. What is there to say? Our lives are so far apart. One small child is asleep curled up in a corner wearing layers of sweaters. His coughing wakes him at intervals. On seeing me he begins to cry - his worst nightmare come true - a white man, or white woman in my case, has invaded his home. Another younger child wakes up and the father holds her in front of the fire to warm her little body. I have walked into a warm, loving family. I am offered a non-descript hot drink but decline their kindness, still worrying about getting diarrhoea

It is a long, long time since the two sisters have been together so there is some awkwardness. The woman explains to me later that this is a very important trip for her - primarily it is to visit her mother's grave and ask for forgiveness - her brother and sister did not, or maybe could not, tell her of the death for months. Blue plastic sheeting is laid out on the ground, sheets and blankets are found for the three visitors. This is our bed. We sleep fully-clothed. It is cold. A soft animal snuggles round my feet, and it is not until morning that I discover it is the cat. I spend most of the night feeling slightly bewildered in my strange surroundings, but very safe. The storm continues outside and occasionally drops of water leak through the thatched roof onto my face. Will I ever reach Rurrenabaque?

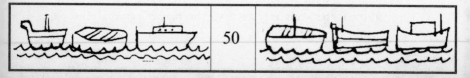

STRANGER IN THE NIGHT.

The night flight from San Francisco to Heathrow had been delayed for
several hours. At last passengers were boarding, crowding onto the plane,
blocking aisles as they stowed bags and baggage and hunted for their seats.
Suddenly the chaos erupted with angry shouts and shrill cries of pain. There
was pandemonium as an enormous man barged his way down the narrow
aisle towards row H, shoving aside everyone and everything in his path.
The window seat beside me was still unoccupied.

"Oh no!" I prayed. "Please no!" But yes.

"I find my seat!" he announced in triumph and promptly set about
trying to push past my friend, Joan, seated beside me in the aisle slot. All her
agonised squeals as well as the urgent pleas of an irate stewardess to let us
out first were ignored. Joan managed to escape into the aisle considerably
dishevelled but undamaged. I was not so lucky, trapped in the middle seat.

"Wait!" I yelled, trying to rescue my duty-frees and my feet from
destruction by clambering onto the seat. My desperate cries were stifled by
the vast trousered rump pressing into my face. I should have taken a vicious

bite while there was the chance.

"I find my seat", the odious creature repeated with pride, flashing a mouthful of gold teeth as he squeezed his flesh into his allotted space, every inch of him not constrained by the arm-rest bulged over into my barely adequate seat.

"How this go up?" He asked, tugging at the arm-rest.

"It doesn't!" I snap, clamping my hand on it with a glare. He was gross; middle-aged and oily with swarthy pocked-marked skin, a large Levantine nose and thick slobbery lips: definitely not my type; positively yucky. He caught me looking.

"Dr. Mohammed from Cairo, Egypt," he beamed. Gold flashed. "And you?" He waited expectantly. I pretended not to hear.

There was no snubbing Dr. Mohammed. He repeated the question adding, "You English?"

A curt, "No." Then relenting - after all one must be polite to foreigners, "Scottish."

That stumped him. I explained, "From Scotland."

It was obvious he had never heard of Scotland. He was silenced temporarily.

As the plane began to move, he grabbed my hand in a vice-like grip resisting my struggles to get free.

"Pliss! I fright." He pleaded, pale and trembling, sweating profusely. It was his first flight. He had travelled to the States by sea and crossed by coach to San Francisco to visit his surgeon brother. So I held his hand, scandalising Joan. What else could I do?

I extricated my hand from his clammy paw as soon as the plane levelled out. He had calmed down.

Dr. Mohammed refused a drink from the drinks trolley explaining that his religion forbade alcohol.

'That nice?" He eyed my whisky, then reached across and snatched it from my tray. It vanished in one gulp.

"I like!" He announced, returning the empty glass.

Speechless with outrage, I couldn't raise a squeak of protest - nor another drink. Worse was to come.

The unwanted rolls and gooey desserts were grabbed from our dinner trays with, "You no want. I eat." Having wolfed those, he struggled to his feet, sending all three trays flying, and howled for a stewardess to bring more food. The Captain of the plane, on his rounds of the cabin, hurried to investigate the disturbance, and gave grudging permission for a second foil-wrapped meal to be served to Dr. Mohammed.

"Are you ladies all right?" he asked. "I'm sorry the plane is full so we can't move you to other seats."

Not as sorry as I was. This gross stranger was destined as my sleeping partner. I had heard rumours, but learned first hand just how intimate things could be in the darkened cabin of a jumbo.

Dr. Mohammed's size meant we were unavoidably in contact, arm to arm, thigh to thigh, but his hands didn't have to wander. First they reached across me to remove Joan's pack of duty free cigarettes from the pocket in front of her. I retrieved them with a hissed threat to have him thrown off the plane by the Captain. That worked for a time, but I soon grew tired of pushing his hands off my person saying "Stop it!" At last the Mogadon I took earlier won and I fell into an uneasy sleep wondering what he might try next.

"You have nice sleep?" Dr. Mohammed asked unabashed when I awoke in the morning. He seemed very chirpy, quite unworried at the prospect of landing at the world's busiest airport. No wonder! When I eventually reached home I discovered that the litre bottle of whisky in the duty-free bag I'd stowed under my seat in the plane, had been opened and a good third swiped.

That's what the man had been after! And I'd thought...

EN ROUTE TO ALBANIA.

A few years ago, Albania opened its doors to the rest of the world and I booked one of the first package holidays there. Being a middle aged matron and usually travelling alone, I always think that better results are achieved if one is better dressed and as a result my suitcases are usually enormous. I am the kind of traveller who takes twelve T-shirts when staying for a week, and am most unhappy if I can't take several hair appliances. On this occasion I did not think that Albania would require my 'Come Dancing' evening wear.

Because of the enormous suitcase I opted to take the Wolverhampton-Gatwick Express. No fighting across London. Once on the train at Wolverhampton I could safely relax until the flight at 2.15 pm...or so I thought.

"Due to a breakdown further up the line...!"

We move one hundred yards up the line. A small boy is playing in the garden of a nearby house. We wave and smile at each other .

On the train there are signs of unrest. The guard strides purposefully down the train, avoiding eye contact. Time passes. I am not worried. I always leave plenty of time. I am paranoid about it. I am never late.

"We are having problems moving the train in front of us off the line..."

Small signs of unrest begin to surface in my well ordered life. I go to the window and lean out. "Young man," I call the small boy "can you ask your mother to make a telephone call for me please? I will pay for the call and give you some pocket money".

The small chap trots up the narrow garden and into the house. He returns.

"My nan says No." Oh well, well tried!

At last the train moves to the next stop. A group of us wondered whether to clamber across the track and get a taxi. The train moves another ten yards. A lynching party gets ready for the conductor. The train moves again. This time it moves five hundred yards and into the station.

"This train will terminate here. All passengers wishing to go to Gatwick, please go to Platform 2".

We get off the train and wait. A train enters the station.

Arriving at Gatwick I rush to the check-in desk to be told the plane is on the runway and I have missed it.

I weep. I plead. I am prepared to run down the runway and enter the plane via the luggage compartment. I am told I can only go to Albania now via Switzerland. But then that is not possible as my name is on a group visa which is dated that day....

I make plans to return home. I lug my suitcase onto the Gatwick Express. At Euston Station I make my way to the train that is leaving in three minutes. I hand my ticket to a small dark fellow. "You cannot get on this train... you are not eligible..."

At this point all reason departed. Euston was filled with a bright light and ringing bells.

"GET OUT OF MY WAY" I snarl.

"No, you cannot get on this train..."

"DON'T YOU DARE STOP ME, YOU LITTLE S... I'VE HAD ENOUGH OF BRITISH RAIL TODAY!"

...And with one swipe I hit him with my handbag. He stumbles to the ground. I step over him triumphantly, deliberately making sure the wheels of my suitcase gouged his calf as I board the train.

I must confess that I expected the Railway Police to board at every station and it was only when the ticket collector took my ticket and said it was suitable for the trip did I relax.

I did eventually get to Albania. The men were proud and medieval in their outlook. They walked in twos and threes along the streets of Torana, Vlora and Durres, in their shiny brown suits, while the women worked in the fields. They were paranoid about invasion. The food was appalling. Alcohol cheap and pungent. (Where else would you get two bottles of wine and six orange liqueurs for £2.49! It's my round!) Bossy women they didn't like - I know because they told me. (We do not like women like you - they said, when I organised the end of holiday party!)

ARREST IN BUDAPEST.

I've never been arrested in the U.K. but it seems to have become a habit overseas!

I was in Budapest and a group of us were travelling to the city centre by tram when I suddenly realised I was missing my handbag. It had everything in it; my money, my credit cards, my passport. I called to my friend that I was going back to the hotel, and as I leapt onto a tram going in the opposite direction she thrust some money into my hand.

A man approached me. He pulled down the top of his sleeve revealing a military looking red sash. It suddenly dawned on me that he was the ticket inspector. Having been so concerned about my handbag, I had forgotten to punch my ticket as I should when I had got on the bus.

Reluctantly I held out my ticket book. I tried to explain, but he was having none of it. He went through my used tickets one by one. Everyone in the tram was staring. My humiliation peaked when they stopped the tram and I was escorted off by the inspector. I prayed that the earth would open up.

I had only gone to Budapest for five days. I knew not one word, except "Paprika", and a red spice was not going to help me much now. I tried to explain my tale of woe again. But it was too late. I realised that I was going to be fined, a no mean feat without a purse! The yellow ticket he had written out said "five hundred florins"; there was no getting out of it. Suddenly I remembered that my friend had stuffed a note into my hand - I searched for it and pulled out my crumpled offering. The inspector gave me a funny look, took the money gently, then handed me the yellow ticket and let me back on the tram.

I was relieved to leave the humiliation of the tram and get back to the hotel. My bag hadn't been handed in at reception. I ran up several flights of stairs to my room; my bag was not there. Heaving for breath, I rushed into the dining room where we had had breakfast. There, hanging on the back of my seat was my handbag, untouched and in full view of everyone. My surge of relief turned to a surge of guilt for the totally unreasonable view of Hungary that had been so real to me only seconds before.

I got into a third tram that morning and immediately stamped my ticket. Sighing with relief, I looked up and could not believe my eyes - it was the same ticket inspector again! One guide book says ticket inspectors are so rare that you can practically travel in Budapest for free. Embarrassed, I peered out of the corner of my eye to see where he was. It seemed that he had been waiting to greet me. Without pausing to check my ticket, he smiled and nodded to me like an old friend. I smiled back, more in shock than anything.

..And my souvenir from this holiday? ...Yes, a yellow ticket from Budapest!

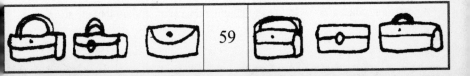

NEW YEAR IN THE ANTARTIC.

My time in the Antarctic was like no other experience - it was absolutely overwhelming. I flew into Punta Arenas, the most Southerly town in Chile and quite rightly known as the bottom of the world. Winds are often so fierce there that you have to fight your way against them to move forward even a few centimetres and always with the prospect of being blown backwards. If the wind is behind you, it propels you forwards so you can't help but gallop down the street at an ever increasing pace. You see people all over Punta Arenas hanging onto trees, railings and lamp posts!

From here it was a six hour flight from our base camp at Patriot Hills. The snow was many colours and variations of greens, blues and white, even reds and oranges as the very bright sun tinged everything in sight.

The major reason I was in the Antarctic was to reach the South Pole. Each day I asked if it was time, only to be told that the winds were too strong, the visibility too poor, the journey too dangerous for all kinds of reasons.

At last on January 1st, I was told that there might be a window the next day and to be prepared. We had to take a large tent, our sleeping bags and enough food for two weeks... just in case! We flew for three hours to a fuelling base called White Fields, then on for another three hours until we finally arrived at the South Pole.

What a magnificent and heroic sight! I stood where the great polar explorers Amundsen and Scott had stood and I photographed the flags of the many nations who have agreed, at least for the time being, to share control of the South Pole and Antarctica. We were then taken around the USA station by the programme director of the National Science Foundation who introduced us to the bushy haired, somewhat strange looking team members who eyed us hungrily - and they were just the women! the men were too busy playing pool and watching videos to do more than wave an acknowledgement. It's all 'hush hush' research, the director explained, tapping his nose mysteriously. The base is built underground, busting with stores, equipment, computers, a large library, a non-stop dining hall, communal mess room and spacious sleeping quarters.

Sadly several hours later it was time to return. We flew for another six hours before arriving back at Punta Arenas, and after a few hours sleep, three more flights, and over twenty hours of flying, I was back in England, but my heart was still in Antarctica.

MESSING ABOUT ON THE RIVER.

I will not bore the reader with the long account of the tedious, day-to-day difficulties; the freezing hotel rooms, pre-historic buses, closed museums, all-night vigils in railway stations, ten hour queues for train tickets and being turned away from hotels late at night. I will refrain from describing at length the more dramatic episodes; the frightening attack by monkeys in the mountains, being rescued then ripped off by soldiers, being hi-jacked by hotel touts and my boat running aground on rocks in the river below Xinping. I mention these things merely to set the scene, so that you may imagine my state of mind six weeks into the trip. Demoralised, exhausted, and, in two words, fed up!

By now I was tired of "authentic" travel experiences. I was beginning to dream of home, of flush toilets, clean sheets, gas fires, hot water and pelican crossings. However, I was confident that the final stage of my journey would be a doddle! As a well-deserved treat, I paid out a small fortune to travel down the Yangtse, from Chongqing to Wuhan in a luxury tourist boat.

Three days of cruising followed by a sleeper train back to Hong Kong. What could be more relaxing? I arrived at the dock area, lugging my heavy rucksack. Three hours to go. I settled down to wait at Wharf 6, enjoying the winter sunshine.

People kept pointing at the wharf and shaking their heads at me. Someone mimed ripping up my ticket. I trudged wearily to an official-looking kiosk and showed him my ticket - he pointed me back to where I'd come from. By now I was becoming resigned to the possibility of being stuck in Chongqing for the rest of my life!

Eventually, a vast iron hulk of a boat moored up! Hundreds of people streamed on board, carting their crates of chickens and yoked sacks of rice. My friends ushered me up the gangplank and into a dormitory in the hold - filthy mattresses, a leaking sink, rusty iron floor and no port-holes. I spent three days and nights in this smoke-filled chicken-coup, as we shuddered and creaked our way downstream, stopping at every little town. The famous scenery of the Three Gorges? Oh yes, we saw them - at night!

Yes I did have a residual pang of disappointment, but China was teaching me a more fatalistic philosophy!

RICE KNIFE.

The bus was supposed to arrive at 7.00 am. It was early - five hours early! My girlfriend and I were dropped off bleary-eyed, several kilometres outside Probolinggo, a small town on the eastern tip of Java. There were no buses, no hotel, no street lights. There was, rather conveniently, a tourist information office, and, despite the fact that it was 2 o'clock in the morning, it was open. Inside a man offered advice of how to get to Mount Bromo - the nearby volcano we intended to climb. The advice was this: a couple of my mates will drive you there and charge you 10 times the going rate for doing so. We laughed and tried to haggle him down, but he started to get aggressive, insisting that in this remote location (and at this god awful hour) we had no choice. We refused to pay and went outside into the pitched black to wait for the next bus.

Then things started to get nasty.

Rocks and stones started to rain down on us from the direction of the tourist office, where 4 or 5 men had been hanging around smoking cigarettes and looking shifty. One of them whipped out a bloody great big rice knife and started pacing up and down, waving the blade in front of us. Then the lights in the tourist office went off. As my eyes started to adjust to the near solid darkness, I could make out the other men starting to put on Balaclavas.

It was one of those brown trouser moments! I had experienced it once before in London when I had gone for a late night wee in a dark alley and bumped into an irate and very tall football supporter who accused me of trying 'to cop a look at his tackle' and threatened 'to pull my bladder out through the end of my own penis'. That time I beat a hasty, if slightly damp, retreat. This time I had a back-pack and a girlfriend to worry about.

We started walking slowly away, waiting for a knife in the ribs, or an extra large rock on the head. Not for the last time on my travels I came over all religious. As if in answer to my prayers, out of the darkness a Becak (a pedal powered taxi) appeared. We flagged it down, threw ourselves and our back-packs on board and waved money at the driver. "Get us out of here fast!" we implored him. We didn't move. On closer inspection our saviour turned out to be a dwarf. Brilliant. Here we were, about to get carved up, and our getaway driver could barely reach the pedals.

I got out and gave him a push start and somehow the little man got us to the safety of the all-night bus depot in town. Relief! We had escaped!

It was then that I realised my treasured Nikon, which had been slung around my neck, was missing.

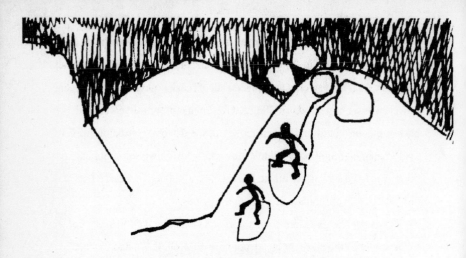

WHITE POWDER HEAVEN.

It had all started so quietly and peacefully that day. It looked as if a snowboarder's dream was becoming true. An untouched powder glacier without anyone else to bother you. We were up for the maximum adventure thrill and I could feel my adrenaline flowing. The mountain was ours and we were flying down about thirty miles an hour. It had become a little windy and the surface of the snow was moving. I was kicking up all this spray every time I did a turn, which would make a massive wave that was instantly blown away. It looked spooky, it was spooky, but it was one of the best experiences I have had in my entire life.

All of sudden, a huge section of the glacier above us broke off. It was a stupidly big block of ice and it exploded when it hit the bottom of a rock a hundred and fifty yards behind us. Besides the Canary Wharf bomb it was the loudest thing I have ever heard in my life. Struck by the shock we could not move. The avalanche caused by the ice block bellowed towards us really fast. We just stood and watched in awe. My life flashed before me. I panicked. I thought "this is it".

By then the avalanche had reached us and masses of snow just roared down over us. Our faces were planted down in the snow .... but we survived! The avalanche did not bury us alive. Death was near, and my first thoughts were that I would never touch a snow board again. We looked at each other for a long moment, both unable to speak a word. These seconds I will surely never forget in my entire life.

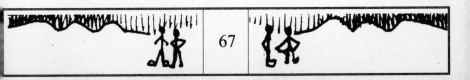

CORPSES AND STRAWBERRIES.

"A jewel in the ocean at the foot of India," the guide book said. Well, that much was true. What nobody had said-at the travel agents, on the aeroplane, or in the media, was that the fighting in Sri Lanka was about to escalate out of control! The embassy had said that all action was restricted to the north, where they were playing (Tamil) Tigers and Indians.

The itinerary went out of the window! Many of the places that I'd planned to visit were now unsafe. "Can't go there, J V P." I was told whenever I tried to purchase a rail ticket or hire a car. The J V P are one of the main rebel groups operating mostly south of the capital. They meant business. They targeted special groups in their attempt to bring the country to a standstill. Bus drivers were an early casualty. One evening all the television news readers disappeared, the army was sent in. The end result was like a sketch from the "Not the Nine O'clock News". On this visit luxury was mine for the asking!

The tourist trade had been decimated. Tour groups had cancelled. Lone travellers, better informed than me, had stayed away. They were desperate for trade, you could barter with everyone. I was invited to the Colombo Hilton later that week, to a strawberry festival...well, strawberries were in season...in England! As I stepped out of my air-conditioned taxi, I noticed a man dressed as a strawberry. Five pounds of English money and you could have a night at the Hilton - ten pounds and they would throw in a five-course dinner! I developed an unfortunate penchant for luxury which has not been compatible with the rest of my life!

Only once did it get hair-raising. Driving in a hired car, we were stopped at gun point by members of the J V P, dressed Rambo-style. "We will borrow your car for ten minutes," they informed us. We sat by the roadside. Exactly ten minutes later the car reappeared. "You will take this letter and drive to the nearest army barracks," the voice behind the gun said. We did. When the letter was read and the boot opened, there was a dead Indian soldier inside.

Looking back, I do not believe I saw much of the real Sri Lanka. My contrasts were not just those usually associated with the Indian sub-continent; wealth and poverty. Sure, that was there in abundance, but my contrasts were more surreal. Of enjoying champagne brunches for the sole reason that at that moment someone was being shot...of shadowy figures emerging from doorways in small villages, whispering, "Come inside. J V P declare a new curfew .They shoot." But the image nailed to the forefront of my memory is still of that Englishman dressed as a strawberry, while all around him his adopted country was tearing itself to pieces.

SERIOUS MONKEY BUSINESS.

Never work with animals or children, the old cliché goes. A statement I firmly believe back-packers should heed, and limit their zoological forays to sitting atop a gaily painted elephant or feeding crocs from the safety of an indigestible metal boat deck. If, like me, you persist further, be warned by the following cautionary tale.

Even more common than cats or dogs in India are the local monkeys. They sit idly in Delhi streets, chatter nosily in parks and live in huge communities like the one on the hills surrounding Jaipur. Even more prolific than cats, dogs or monkeys are carpet sellers, who ply you with the local strange brew whilst trying to flog you their wares.

Ellie, my travelling companion, and I had just experienced the carpet showroom piss-up before going on to look at Jaipur's anarchic monkey troupe. Hundreds of monkeys swarmed over the hills, tugging and tweaking each other and as their curiosity grew, us! One started shaking my hand. Soused to incomprehension, I happily stood there as the sweet little monkey schizophrenically transformed into a ferocious man-eater and joyfully sank its teeth into my hand. I screeched, the monkey scarpered and our guide started moaning to Allah about rabies infections.

Consulting a medical book I read the only method to detect rabies in an animal was to catch it, kill it, remove it's brain and send it to a lab for analysis. A tad impractical, as even in a select ID parade I'd never spot my monkey, let alone be capable of murder. The alternative was to embark upon a series of anti-rabies injections that would lessen the probability of a fatal attack. Shots would be needed at exact times throughout the next two months.

Shot 1 was administered at Jaipur's main hospital, it cost five pounds.

Indian people needing even simple operations have to borrow relatively huge amounts from money-lenders and work for years to pay it off.

My fears about mortality calmed, Ellie and I continued on our exploration of Rajasthan with strict instructions to seek out local hospitals for an injection on designated days. Shots 2 and 3 passed off straight forwardly, though I did receive a white hair fright on returning from a three day camel trek. I' d gotten minor sunstroke and was lying in the hostel bunk room later when I started trembling uncontrollably. "And when the shakes start you know rabies is kicking in" boomed an American voice from behind a bunk. "A horrific death is inevitable" it taunted! Luckily nothing happened and I remained distinctly alive.

Shot 4 was the most mouthdryingly, palpitatingly terrifying day of my life. We'd ended up on a remote island. Cycling to the nearest hospital, we arrived to find it shut. No amount of histrionics could induce the staff to administer the needed shot. Panicking slightly, we cycled furiously back to the small village chemist. He spoke no English and only laughed as I re-enacted the monkey biting scene. Apprehensively I vaulted the counter and started tearing through the contents of his fridges. One lunch and no luck later, I gave up. The nearest town was twenty miles away, on the mainland, and I had to have the shot that day or the whole inoculation process would be useless.

Mildly hysterical by now, we hitched a lift in a cart towed by a huge honky tonk motorised trike. We found a drugstore and again rudely started rooting through their supplies. Praise be. I found the holy shot; but the chemist looked blank when I bared my arm and handed him the needle. With only a Brownie first-aid badge to my credit I wasn't prepared to accidentally pump the gloop into a fatally incorrect spot. On instruction, we hightailed it down dubiously grubby side streets in search of a Doc.

Sweet relief almost choked me as an equally confused 'Doc' injected the vaccine.

Terror subsided and was replaced by the wonder of life. I'll never know if the anti-rabies injections saved my life, but my advice is still to pack thick snake handling gloves, or limit your animal antics to a day pass at London zoo!

MACAWS AND CAPYBARAS ON THE RIO HONDO.

There is a rule of travelling that says you have to suffer if you are to truly appreciate the good things that happen to you, and there are times when I think that is true.

If I had made my trip into the Bolivian Amazon on an expensive tour, with air conditioned accomodation and all meals provided, maybe I would have seen the same things, but it was the fact that I had done it all myself that made the experience so special.

I had carried the canoe, rolled up in my rucksack complete with poles, across the mountains for four days, paddled and dragged it up the river and nearly lost everything when it got swamped in the surging white water of a rapid!

When we made camp on that sixth afternoon, our spirits were low. Much of the food was soaked, despite being double-wrapped in plastic bags, and when we tried spreading it out on the rocks by the river to dry, it attracted swarms of small, black sweat bees that burrowed into the piles of soggy porridge oats and crawled all over the rice. As we couldn't afford to waste rations, that same rice would have to be our meal for the night. By late afternoon, with nothing to do but wait for the food to dry (and hopefully for the bees to disperse), I took the canoe for a paddle upstream.

A gentle splash to my left side jerked me into alertness as three capybaras, two adults and a young one, sidled into the water and swam alongside the canoe. Disappearing under the boat with a 'tuk-tuk' call of alarm as the shrieking calls of four macaws erupted from a riverside tree. A blaze of deepest red, their crimson plumage highlighted in the yellow rays of the late afternoon sun, almost glowed against the shade of the forest beyond. The capybaras surfaced on the other side of the river, first just the eyes and nostrils, and then, when they were sure it was safe, they lifted the rest of their lumpish bodies and stood still for a moment, water streaming from their coarse, slicked-back fur. Then they turned and scuttled into some bushes, just as another flock of macaws burst out noisily across the river, (pursuing the first group). The macaws headed straight for the forested ridges of the headwaters where I knew our journey upstream would take us.

Seeing the capybaras, the macaws and the rising ridges of rainforest laid out so clearly ahead, suddenly made the effort of the trek worthwhile. I remembered what had inspired me to travel up the river and I now knew why I would carry on. With one moment of sheer perfection like that, I could even put up with the thought of picking out the insects from my boiled rice that night!

ONE VIEW FROM THE AIR.

1980. We were young and excited, and after a week in Florida, Jane and I were boarding a flight from Orlando to Washington DC to 'do the sights' there. It was Friday 13th. Neither of us were superstitious, in fact, being on holiday, we were hardly aware of the date.

As we took our seats near the back of the aircraft, we noticed that some had been removed and a coffin slotted in the space.

Across the aisle from us was the traditional fat American family: Dad and Mom with Little Fatty stuffing his face with sweets. A coca cola can was held in his spare hand. Diagonally in front was a business man. He already had his briefcase open and was scribbling in a notebook and drawing diagrams of some sort.

We sat in the plane waiting for lift-off. A long black limousine drew up and a woman dressed in black was helped out. We could hear her weeping and wailing about how she wanted to die, she had no reason to live any longer. Jane and I looked at each other. This must be the widow of the coffin occupant. She, and her two supporters, were seated right behind us.

Finally we had lift-off. Little Fatty opened a second can of coca cola and started on the crisps. The business man opened more books and continued to scribble. The widow behind accepted a large gin and continued to weep and wail loudly about how life wasn't worth living. Jane and I pored over our tourist brochures and planned what we wanted to see in Washington.

Half an hour into the flight, the pilot announced turbulent weather ahead. A few minutes afterwards, the plane hiccuped in a thermal. Jane and I grinned at each other.

"Just like Disney World, hey?" We commented loudly in our best of

British voices. The stewardess came round and started checking all seats were upright. The pilot suggested everyone sat down and fastened seat belts.

"How frightfully exciting," quipped I, really laying on the British accent. The plane starting lurching and heaving around the sky. Beneath us we could see thick black thunder clouds.

The business man put away his papers and took out a small book which looked like a Bible. He was reading, his lips moving but no sound coming out.

Little Fatty turned a shade of grey and started throwing up. A stewardess was summoned by Mom. The poor stewardess couldn't squeeze past Mom and Dad to reach Little Fatty who by now had thrown up most of the coca cola and sweets he had eaten. They had to change seats, carefully trying to avoid the pool of vomit round their feet. The smell slowly seeped round the aircraft. Little Fatty asked for another Coke to take the taste away.

The Weeping Widow behind us had gone quiet. One of her supporters asked for a large bourbon and more gin. As the plane lurched, there was a sliding sound and the coffin moved forward to rest against the back of their seats. Someone screamed.

Jane and 1 giggled and whooped with each swoop of the plane. The turbulence finally ended and the flight calmed down. The stewardesses sold their drinks and dished out food. Then we started the long slow descent. The Captain made an announcement.

"We seem to have an hydraulic failure, folks. We'll have to make an emergency landing. The stewardesses will now go through the emergency procedures again. Please watch them closely." Jane and I looked at each other. This was really exciting. We asked a stewardess what an hydraulic failure meant as she came round checking seat positions and belts.

"The wing flaps can't be operated and the wheels have to be lowered manually, ma'am," she explained for the umpteenth time.

"I say, this is really exciting," Jane and I enthused.

The businessman had his Bible out again and was now openly praying, his voice carrying several rows. Quite a few people joined in his Amens. The Weeping Widow called for more gin, declaring she didn't want to die yet. Little Fatty slurped up another can of coca cola and started whining to Mom and Dad to let him sit back beside the window.

Jane and I watched, exclaiming in our best British voices about the fire engines and ambulances that lined the runway as we did a low circle before landing. The ambulances and fire engines raced alongside the aircraft as we taxied along the runway, tyres screeching and engine screaming as the Captain did whatever he could to slow us down.

We were so disappointed when the plane came safely to a halt. Loudly we complained about not needing to use the emergency exits, slide down the slide, or be rescued by handsome firemen or doctors.

The business man was loudly proclaiming a prayer of thanks; Little Fatty, Mom and Dad were already standing and trying to avoid the remains of the pool of vomit by their feet as they tried to pull their baggage from the overhead storage; the Weeping Widow was helped to her shaky feet and slurred through the gin that she just wanted to go home. Jane and I declared it one of the most exciting flights we'd ever taken and thanked the stewardess as we left the aircraft, trying to keep up our British stiff upper lip and accent as we walked through the obviously ruffled Americans.

'NAM HELL WITH ANGELS.

It was night, it was Vietnam and I was suddenly jolted awake by a scream from the front of the overcrowded local bus. The world spun and I was thrown face down into cold, dark, muddy water, pinned there by the weight of luggage and people on top of me.

To panic was to drown. I had to stay calm, I reasoned that the bus had stopped moving. I was alive. I could think. I could hold my breath for two minutes. It was only a matter of time before people got off me and removed the luggage.

I waited. It was a long wait. A wait where hope was centre stage with terror hovering in the wings, poised for that anticipated, choking, suffocating and final gasp.

Gasp! But it was air. A wiry Vietnamese man was standing over me, my lips just above the water line. I moved and discovered the bus was lying on my arm. He tried to heave me up. "My arm, my ARM!!" I screamed. He didn't understand, but he could hear the pain. He quickly ran his hands over me to ascertain where I was trapped and spent 10 minutes trying to pull me out on his own. Eventually, another man came to help and centimetre by centimetre, my arm was released, minus bracelets and a fair bit of skin. I was alive and free, not everyone was so lucky.

The next six days in hospital were difficult. No one spoke English; the bed was a ridged board; water came from a well. People arrived in droves just to stare at me. Chickens and cockroaches wandered in and out of my room; I didn't know what medication I was being given. The loo was unmentionable. My mind was replaying the crucial few seconds over and over. I had lost virtually everything, including three professional cameras.

I smile when I think back, though, because I remember the over whelming kindness I was shown by the hospital staff; meals I was given by women in the village; invitations to their homes; old women who visited me in hospital (even though they didn't speak, they sat in silence offering moral support and then left); they loved to comb my strange red hair. There was a genuine concern from everyone for my well-being and whilst I felt I was in hell, in reality I was with angels.

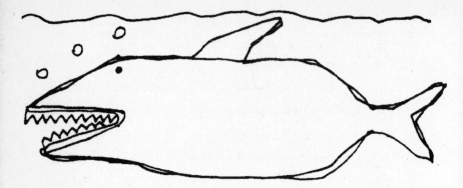

TALLOW'S BEACH.

I was taking a breather - resting on my board. You cannot imagine how crystal clear the water was! It was amazing! I looked around for shells hidden in the sand on the sea bed. I was wondering if I could touch the bottom. It always looks shallower than it really is. The next thing I knew was a girl shouting "SHARK!" I turned around to face a black fin rising up out of the water - and in my direction! My first reaction was to take my arms and legs out of the water. The next thing I know a sleek, black, twelve foot shadow is gliding beneath me. Its evil-looking mouth was surrounded with spikes - it is what I understand to be Tiger Shark. If I thought I was short on adrenaline, it soon came back, pumping full force through my veins. I could hear my heart pumping and I had never appreciated the wondrous gift of life so much. The fear of death had suddenly become something very tangible.

Well, I guess you know I made it back.... I lived to tell the tale! I guess people kind of exaggerate stories like these, but .... it was twelve foot long - I swear on my life !!

A BULLET FOR YOUR THOUGHTS.

In a couple of days, I had experienced two unrelated incidents of guns being used in anger. The first was witnessing a boy of seventeen or eighteen being murdered by two civilians on the street. Now it was my turn to be on the receiving end and I was terrified.

The Pan American highway divided with no indication of which way Peru was, and which was the way to the cold hostile Andes. The compass rather than instinct won, and the pitted road soon became more pit than road. Picking my way through the puddles of indeterminable depth, I became aware of two men standing behind scrubby thorn bushes which skirted the road to my right. Maybe all my revving and wheel spin had attracted their attention, but soon they were only about twenty feet away, still partly obscured by the shrubbery. Normally in such a remote part, a gesture of friendship would have been appropriate, but my hands were too busy and a full face helmet is not conducive to conversation.

The taller one with a weather beaten face and a broad rimmed hat, raised an arm to point at the ridiculous white man, fighting to keep vertical on his big bike. The next few seconds were the longest of my life. An ear shattering bang and windscreen fragments hitting my visor happened simultaneously. It wasn't until I heard the second explosion and suffered a sensation like being kicked very hard just behind and above my right ear that I became convinced that it was a hand gun and not a finger pointing at me.

Adrenaline tried to take over, but curiously enough the part of my brain still functioning pleaded caution. I managed to accelerate away from the brink of disaster. The next mile went on for a life time. There was no acute pain, just a deep bass note throb following me. My vision was blurred but probably due to tears and a steamed up visor rather than anything dramatic. My shaking limbs still responded to every bump in the road as the hideous truth slowly sank in. I had to stop and check the damage, to confirm my head was still where it used to be and confirm I was still alive and not riding as a headless chicken runs.

Amazingly a rational composure took over once the bike was safe. Wrenching the crash helmet off took a concerted effort and a good deal of cursing. My reflection in a wing mirror revealed nothing as the wound was too far back. Gently probing with quivering fingers I found hair matted with dry blood. It was obvious my injury was minor. I forced my helmet over a throbbing wound and rode off with ringing in my ears. The fear of armed bandits pursuing was the only reason I needed to get the hell out of there.

There is one question that still nags me while suffering the irritation of insomnia, why was there not a third shot?

Ecuador never held the magical beauty of Columbia to me but from that day on, my eyes absorbed the naked rusty mountains with affection as the realisation of human frailty smacks me in the face - or should I say hit me in the back of the head.

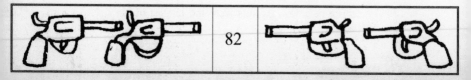

REMEMBERING.

There was a time once, a place, somewhere along the Moroccan / Algerian border. I don't know where it was - perhaps it doesn't matter. The sky was deepest velvet black and the stars glowed an iridescent brilliant white. Right above us was the milky way, a semi circle hovering like an iridescent rainbow; the stars individual, each unique, yet veiled within an aura of translucent white mesh, hovering amongst the elements.

At this military base, the guards welcomed us warmly. We shared no common language, yet it did not matter. They were pleased at human company. We were pleased at nature's company. We sat, in silence, around the embers of the fire which was spitting softly and glowing warmly. The night was cold, fresh, energising. It gave life and peace to us now in our unique place in our own histories and in the history of those we meet and of the places we visit.

I lay on the desert sand, looking up at the stars, feeling the natural energy around me. I fingered the sand between my fingers, letting it spill grain by grain. It flowed like water to the ground, nature back to nature.

These times assume a sacred place in our memories of travel. We are here, wherever that may be, and we become part of history's natural cycle. We are as much or as little as that.

ONLY FOOLS AND HORSES.

"Let's hire some horses and ride out into the desert!"

Maybe the romance of the pyramids in Egypt made us get a little carried away with the moment. I had clean forgotten I had never ridden a horse before but it "seemed like a good idea at the time". The local man who accompanied us (an Egyptian with a distinct lack of command over the English language) tethered my horse to his for this very reason. My partner on the other hand immediately started to practise his Clint Eastwood manoeuvres, prancing off into the dunes.

At first the journey took on true adventure, as we cantered far away from the tourist trappings, to a different world of hidden villages and lush oases, where women and children secretly bathed. The date and palm trees along the shady lanes soon gave way to endless tedious desert, and we started to pass bemused tourists on a motley collection of donkeys, camels and horses traipsing back from where we were heading! The 'one hour canter' turned into a five hour marathon as it took two and a half hours to get out to the sunken pyramids. More pressing matters, in every sense of the word, took on greater importance, namely the soreness and discomfort from the bony frames of the horses on our posteriors. In addition our guide had a habit of cantering ahead with me helplessly attached, leaving my partner far behind; he had long since dumped the Clint Eastward heroics and became increasingly concerned for my safety. We gave each other reassuring grimaces - was I to be whisked off to the white slave market? I hear they like them plump and white in this part of the world.

As darkness fell we headed home and to say that we were relieved to be back was an understatement.

For the following few days in Cairo, two healthy twenty somethings were reduced to what can only be described as a cross between John Wayne and geriatrics with severe arthritis. As we hobbled around the antiquities found in the Museum of Egypt, we paused every few yards to take a welcome rest from a set of muscles hitherto unknown, but now making themselves extremely evident.

Never mind the curse of King Tut: beware dodgy horse stables bearing the name Giza!

SOME PEOPLE!

Our aim was to get the ferry to Padang. The boat was leaving that lunch-time and we managed to buy our tickets without too much difficulty. Enough time to get something to eat and to stock up on a few snacks for the journey.

Unfortunately we met a couple we vaguely knew and were talked into going for some 'Padang food' with them. There was a wide variety of plates of different bits and pieces, including chicken, fish, eggs and the inevitable rice. The idea was to eat what you wanted off the dishes and you would be charged for that - the remainder was put back for the next customer. I know these things have to be tried, but I must admit I found the food absolutely revolting - Oh, what would I have done for a plate of chips or a tin of baked beans!

When we went to pay we found they wanted to charge us an extortionate price which we haggled down slightly, but we ended up having to pay most of it in the end. This all took so much time that we had to rush straight back to catch the boat, still hungry and without getting supplies for the thirty hour trip!!

The couple who had enticed us to eat this food were pretty dreadful - 'the hardened travellers', the kind who had done everything before we had, seen more and done it cheaper and therefore experienced everything 'in a better way' than we had. Of course they had booked fifth class seats on the boat which were right down at the bottom where your bed was a hard board in a room you shared with about a hundred others at least, coughing and spitting all over the place, being sick everywhere and babies wailing their heads off. Then they proceeded to tell us that this was 'sheer luxury' compared with all their past hardships on other journeys. Call us softies, but we thought we would pay the extra fifty pence each and so had splashed out on fourth class tickets.

Every meal was the same and all as revolting as each other - boiled rice, odd-looking vegetables if you can call them that, with spicy fish heads. Breakfast, dinner, tea. We managed to avoid our hardened traveller couple who no doubt would have eaten worse before and would have considered this to be a luxurious banquet.

DO I LIKE CAU CAU ?

It was eight thirty in the morning and I was scouring the streets of Lima for breakfast. Now my Spanish was not superb, but when I saw a sign saying "Cafe, Pan y Cau-Cau-2 Soles" I knew it meant Coffee, Bread and - Cau Cau? Hmmm. I wasn't sure but Cau Cau sounds a bit like cocoa doesn't it? So it must be some kind of chocolate. However, at only two Soles it was a bargain. So, sleepily my friend and I wandered into the cafe and ordered. The waitress gave us a very long look and asked us if we were sure. "Of course we are" we replied.

Five minutes later our feast was laid out before us; a big cup of coffee, a crusty roll, and a plate of *curried intestines!* The perfect way to start the day.

HOW TO HITCH-HIKE ACROSS WATER.

Down to five dollars and stranded on a baby sister island of Zanzibar, my only hope was a free ride on a local ferry. Foreigners were supposed to pay twenty five dollars, but the captains were all Norwegian, so I thought I might have a chance.

With very little enthusiasm I was at the ferry terminal by 8.00 am. My depression wasn't helped by an empty stomach. 1 hadn't eaten in two days - I wasn't going to break into my last five dollars bill!

After all the incoming passengers had disembarked, and before any departing ones had begun to board, I met a very surly Chief Officer from Tanga with (so I thought at the time) a serious attitude problem! My fears increased. When I asked him if I could see the Captain privately, I was told that Jan, the Norwegian normally on this run, had been replaced. The name he gave me sounded extremely Tanzanian. My fears increased. Besides - he was taking a bath!

When the Captain had finally finished his ablutions, I was summoned. He was indeed Tanzanian and informed me, firmly and "regrettably", that there was no way he could help me. All I could do was to talk to the company people in the office. My last vestiges of hope disappeared altogether. Desperately I implored him to let me wait untill all the paying passengers were aboard and then, maybe, please? If there was a single square foot of space where I could stand? Could I? Please? He did not react in any way. He looked at me for a long time and then said flatly, "Go! Wait on quay!"

At ten, the scheduled sailing time, the surly Chief motioned me to come aboard. He ordered me to stand outside the door of the Bridge. The boat was already loaded to twice the capacity stated as being licensed to carry, and double the number that could be accommodated in the life-rafts I might add! There were also just as many, with valid tickets still standing on the dock waiting to board!! The closest I managed to get to the Bridge was half way up the companionway!

After a while. I was brusquely ordered to follow the Chief again. He led me to a saloon in the bowels of the ship. As I disappeared deeper and deeper into the ferry's belly, little by little I let myself start to hope again. Not a word had been spoken!

The overcrowding by this time was unbelievable. The saloon I was in was designed to accommodate sixty - it said so on the wall. There were one hundred and five of us! It seemed like there were also as many screaming infants and chickens, and there was never a time during the seven and a half hour crossing when the sound of a hungry, tired, wet and overheated baby could not be heard!

At last, I felt the ship get under way and I allowed myself a further easing of tension. Two extremely uncomfortable hours into the trip I was again summoned by the Chief. Still grim-faced, he bade me come to him in the galley. OK - here we go, I thought. Negotiation time!

No such thing. I was offered a soda, which I accepted without thinking. He then told me to fetch my bag and follow him through the galley, the mess-hall and into a private lounge? I later saw a plate above the door that read "VIP Saloon" Two obese and obviously highly influential gentlemen were already seated inside and were also being served sodas. One of them handed over some money to the steward?? I was confused! I was then told to put my bag up on a shelf behind one of the seats and 'STAY'! I did, and promptly went to sleep, lulled by the motion of the ship and the pulse of her engines and the comfort of a big, soft arm-chair!

Four hours later 1 woke as the same glowering Chief brought us all plates of beef, rice and salad, followed by a banana. I really did not understand any of what was happening. Never once did anyone attempt to offer an explanation. I dreaded the price I was going to be asked to pay for all this!

At last I felt the engines slow. Again the Chief approached, the exact same expression on his face. This time he found some paper and began to scribble furiously. "Right" I thought. "Here comes the bill!" I still have that grubby little piece of paper today. He had written his name. address and telephone number in Zanzibar on it!!!!!!!!!!!!

As I was leaving the ship 1 thanked him from the bottom of my heart. Whereupon his face broke into the most wonderful smile and as we pumped each others' hands he pressed a thousand shillings (two dollars) into my palm!

Oh how wrong can we be sometimes?

CLOSE ENCOUNTER.

The final stage of the journey across Africa was planned to take us west, touching Botswana, before entering Namibia. My companion, Andy, and I had to cross the Caprivi Strip before riding our mountain bikes south-west to our finishing point, Swakopmund, on the Atlantic Ocean. Sixteen hundred tough and desolate kilometres lay ahead over the next three weeks. Temperatures were likely to reach 40 degrees C. Water and food would be scarce. An added problem was the remote nature of this region of Africa. We would be lucky to find the occasional tiny settlement where we could find water. We had decided to be self-sufficient, carrying as much food and water as possible. The consequences of being caught unprepared in such inhospitable terrain were not pleasant.

Leaving behind the ordered civilisation of Victoria Falls we soon found ourselves pedalling through thick bush on a rough sandy track. I retreated into the comfort and security of my thoughts. Here we were, out in the middle of it all. No sense of time, free to do as we wished, no constraints. Great. It was like a game without rules or if there were rules we made them up as we went along. No one had control over us. No one even knew where we were. Andy and I were experiencing a unique sense of total freedom.

After fifty hard kilometres pedalling the bikes through sand we entered Zambezi National Park, internationally famed for its prolific wildlife. I tried to force childhood images of savage carnivores from my mind. The bush was strangely hushed. Not even bird song broke an uneasy silence. There was a sense of expectancy. I waited uneasily for some event over which I would have no control. Despite the fierce heat of the Zimbabwe sun these thoughts sent a shiver down my back.

'I don't like it,' I said to Andy.

He looked at me questioningly, 'What do you mean?'

'I'm not sure, but let's be careful...'

I cruised along fifty metres behind Andy lulled by the gentle, mesmerising whir of my freshly oiled gears. I glanced up as a huge dark shape drifted from deep bush into the road a hundred metres ahead. My eyes widened in astonishment. Andy continued pedalling away, head down, unaware he was about to cycle headlong into several tons of bull elephant! A shout died in my throat. I was too far back to warn him. I could only look on with sickly fascination as he rode on to his destiny.

Instinct caused Andy to look up from his handlebars at the very last moment. The bike skidded sideways as he rammed on the brakes. Man and machine were thrown heavily onto the sandy track. The heavily laden bike continued sliding forwards under its own momentum, shuddering and bouncing with a life and energy all of its own. Rider and bike finally came to a stop right underneath the belly of one of the most dangerous of animals.

Andy lay quite still looking up at a mountain of grey flesh. For what seemed like many seconds there was absolute silence. The great bull peered about him with small rheumy eyes. Time was briefly suspended in a tableau of terror. I saw things with the same slow motion clarity with which I had once witnessed a car crash. The huge beast slowly uncoiled his huge trunk like a massive grey python. His great ears flapped like tattered canvas sails setting up a cloud of white dust. The bull scented the man smell and became agitated, letting out an ear splitting trumpeting cacophony that echoed around the dense bush.

Andy was keeping very still indeed underneath the angry elephant. He finally managed to extricate himself from his bike, got shakily to his knees, steadied himself and shot out from under the bull like a rabbit chased by a Doberman. He found the nearest mopani tree and shot up it, not stopping until he had reached the very top branches.

The elephant, deprived of the object of its displeasure, discovered the bike beneath him and vented his full anger upon its fragile frame. With the powerful trunk, he picked up the machine, raised it high into the air as though it was a piece of straw and smashed it into the ground with stunning force. Not content with this, the beast lifted a huge round foot and brought it crashing down repeatedly onto the bike.

In next to no time the bike was reduced to a mass of twisted black metal. The blood-red panniers had split, spilling pots, pans, tent and a pair of union jack boxer shorts across the track. The bull stood triumphantly over the scene of carnage and lifted his trunk for one last victorious trumpeting blast. Like a spent hurricane the storm was finally over. The bull decided to leave the metal carcass to the vultures. He calmly surveyed the scene of devastation, turned and with a few ponderous steps was swallowed by thick bush.

After several minutes I plucked up the courage to pedal to the spot where Andy had disappeared. I looked up to find my friend clinging desperately to a branch high in the tree. His face had turned chalk-white and he was staring owl-like at the mayhem that had once been his bike.

'I told you it was a jungle out here,' I said breathlessly.

'Bloody hell,' murmured Andy.

TEA TIME IN MEXICO.

I plunged into the Rio Grande and left America. There is a small void, a no man's land between Mexico and America, a place traversed by thousands seeking to achieve their great 'American Dream'. I was going against the tide and heading for an authentic Tex-Mex dinner. For the first time in my life, I was an illegal immigrant.

My co-conspirators were a band of international travellers. Some went two by two in a little boat across to an unknown village, but I preferred to swim there. I dried off on the riverbank and gazed back at America. There were no obvious differences. Reddish brown earth dissolved on either side into the water.

So, time for a drink before dinner! We were led to a bar; a collection of tables on a veranda. I walked up to order a "Carta Blanca" from a small shuttered door and found myself in a kitchen. A family huddled around the kitchen table watching the TV, and the proprietor of this bar walked over to his refrigerator, pulled out a beer and charged me a dollar, and then we went and sat in his garden. Soon we were befriended by the village idiot. More of an eccentric, I guess. He was bare-chested and like Rambo had a bandanna around his head and wore knives and spears in his belt. He rambled in Spanish and we smiled politely and took pictures for the album. We wandered on further for more photographic evidence of this haven just a swim away from the US. Three small children were having a bath in a washing-up bowl outside their house. They grinned at the lens. We noticed little shadows following us on our meanderings around their village. Soon we were dancing around in circles with these little children who were fascinated with our hippy clothes, doc martens and our hi-tech cameras.

Dinner was served. Our chef was in a bit of a tizzy. Unbeknown to us, she had run out of chicken and we were eating goat and she was very worried about it. The rich spices mixed with the sour cream and guacamole around the spicy meat, was washed down with our cold beer. We sat in her garden, surrounded by curious eyes. All too soon it was time to leave Mexico. With belly full, I decided to be rowed back to the States. We waved at the children who saw us off, and then waved at the US Border guards who had heard of our illegal jaunt across the river and wanted to make sure only white faces were coming back to the land of the free. They nodded to us accepting our English accents as authentic, but they didn't tell us to have a nice day. As we all walked back to the bus to tour more of this great continent, we looked back at the Rio Grande and watched the sun set over Mexico.

TREKKERS DELIGHT.

It was just a few days before Christmas and there I was, stretched out, lying under the twinkling stars of a Northern Thailand night sky.

So what was I doing there in the dark, in the dirt, in the middle of the night; my day's companions sleeping, nestling like sardines (things were abit short on the personal space side of things), back in our own little wooden hut built on stilts?

I was sick - sick as a dog, as they say - and it was hell; hell in its finest form as far as I was concerned; there at that very moment. I was more or less convinced that this was it, my time was up and I was going to die, there in the dirt with the croaking frogs and the grunting pigs and the dogs. And somehow at these times (which will be familiar to most travellers!) it never makes any difference whatsoever that somewhere - deep in your sub-conscious, there is a small rational voice saying "don't worry, this won't last long - you will feel better, maybe even tomorrow, and you're not going to die!" When you're too exhausted to move; too weak to try to get back to the albeit relative comfort of your cosy wooden hut and sleeping mat, you just can't help giving serious consideration to the fact that maybe, just maybe, it might have been better to stay home in good old, cold old, England for the winter -at least when you're there you can stay in bed when you're ill!!

But now it's morning and soon the village will be rising and people will be starting their day, so much for any sleep, but at least I'd survived my night-time ordeal and all those fear filled fantasies of "Death in dirt" and "Mauled by mad village pig"- these were all fading away. Now my reality was that it was the start of a new day and that meant another day's hard walk to the next village, the next hut and the next chance for a wash and sleep! It was time to join the human race again!

What seemed like many hours later, we arrived at a beautiful Lahu village, built high up on a hillside . No streams here, but there was a water tap and it had been a hot hard day. It felt great to chuck a bucket of water over myself and then to roll out my bed-mat in our new (this time bamboo) hut, and sleep and sleep and sleep - and that was Heaven!

WHAT A TRUMPET!

It was so black. As I held my hand out in front of my eyes I couldn't even make out its outline, never mind the individual fingers. We crept together, across the sandy ground, the tough grass brushing our legs. We knew that they were near, we could hear faint splashing sounds. It seemed that they were eating and drinking. Finally we were close enough. Our guide signalled to us, and whispered "now".

Simultaneously, our torch lights shone out. Blinking, as we tried to adjust to the light, we were absorbed by the sounds. Forty elephants were stamping across the ground, swimming and trumpeting. The noise surrounded us, pounded through us and slowly faded as they escaped into the distance. Only then, as the show finished, were our eyes adjusting to the light. Letting out a breath, my first since we had illuminated the elephants, I returned with my companions to our sleeping bags and the rest of our kit.

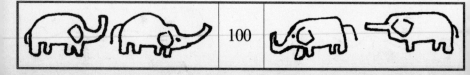

STRANDED.

I was on the island of Martinique in the Winward Islands, the loveliest place that I have ever seen. Flowering trees and shrubs, hosts to the exotic humming birds which were no bigger than ants and could disappear down the throats of Hibiscus flowers. Brilliant butterflies vied with the unfamiliar shells on the beaches and colourful tropical fish swam in the clear water. I explored inland and discovered beaches used by friendly locals, and the myriad of strange trees and wild flowers. I walked to the plantation owned by the Empress Josephine's family where only the sugar mill's chimney remains, and saw her mother's tomb in the ant-eaten church at Trois Ilets. I wondered if she knew that her daughter would end up as Empress of France.

I was longing to get to Diamond Bay on the far side of the island, so when I saw a T.C. labelled for a village about half-way there, I hopped aboard. It was Sunday, and I arrived to find the village 'en fete', with colourful stalls everywhere and folk in their Sunday best. It was fun to categorise the ladies by the points tied in their turban style head dresses... one meant single, two married, and three "I'm available". Frigate birds flew overhead and a rusty hub in the harbour warned of the perils of sea-faring.

The driver dropped me off at a small car park in the village; I could see the beach through the trees, but I needed a cool drink first. I looked for my purse to see how much I had left for lunch.

IT WASN'T THERE!! I scrabbled frantically in my handbag. Nothing. The ground around was fine sand - no purse. What was I going to do, miles from my hotel and without even the price of a phone call?

Suddenly I heard the sound of an engine and the screech of brakes. The T.C. had returned, full of smiling passengers and one of them waving my purse out of the window. My face must have been thanks enough for they barely stayed for me to say thank you before they were off again, waving and smiling!

I was overwhelmed; those people were not rich and there had been a lot of money in my purse. I thanked my guardian angel, zipped up my bag securely, and went in search of a much needed drink.

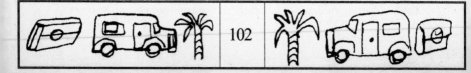

GUNS ROSES AND THE ROAD TO MANDALAY.

The Burmese War had escalated and the chances of me crossing into Myanmar and then Bangladesh to travel overland on half a ton of Triumph, with spare fuel and a mobile workshop, was remote.

After a day of walking around all the shipping offices in astounding humidity with no success, I was condemned to sleep out once more next to my bike on a rubbish tip that passes as a beach. It sounds very romantic, star-gazing at night in a sleeping bag, but in the morning, you clean your teeth with yesterday's flat beer, and you cannot find your clothes - as they are the same colour as the dirt that you are lying in.

In my dishevelled state, I went to a Muslim cafe for Root, a sort of egg pancake served with curry sauce and dhall. While tucking in, I noticed an old Indian tramp on a pavement bench. Under the bench were three plastic bags, bulging with his worldly possessions. Just a few feet past him was my bike, overloaded with just about everything I owned. The cafe fed him, and in turn he shared his meagre meal with a rather mangy looking dog. I identified with this man. Both of us hiding behind unkempt beards, and under long matted hair. Two solitary vagrants with no home, no comfortable bed, and little more than street dirt to stand up in.

He did not beg, but occasionally a passer-by dropped a coin into his hand. He and the dog stopped eating their boiled rice to nod their thanks in a very dignified fashion. The cafe owner took no payment for my Root as it was a gift to a white stranger. Good people, the Malays. Passing the old man's bench, I dropped the one Ringget (about fifty pence and the price of breakfast) into his hand, and patted the dog. He touched his forehead with both hands, then held them together as if in prayer. The thought of his wrinkly smiling face kept my spirits up all the way back to Kuala Lumpur.

A ROMANTIC ENCOUNTER.

Two elderly men sat together in comfortable fireside armchairs, each holding a glass of fine brandy and a cigar. A log fire glowed warmly, its flames throwing flickering shadows on the walls. Rain-dappled windows rattled in the wind. They had been quietly reminiscing all evening and the brandy bottle was almost empty. Inevitably their talk turned to love.

The slightly older one glanced at his friend over the rim of his glass and after a pause said, "George. Tell me about your favourite romance,"there was a slight brandy slur in his voice.

"Romance? My favourite romance?" George stared at the dancing blue and yellow flames and drew lightly on his cigar. He said nothing for a while, immersed deep in thought.

George began hesitantly, "Well.... When we first met it was at the end of a very long journey. I remember I felt very tired and my initial impression wasn't all that good. But... But then I was immediately aware of her warmth. From the very first moment we met, her personality seemed to wrap herself around me."

"Did you know her long?"

"In terms of time, no," replied George. "But, I felt I'd known her all my life. It was obvious that no man could know her, even for a short time and emerge unchanged. I knew immediately that I'd carry an imprint of her forever."

"She was beautiful then?"

George's eyes brightened as he spoke. "At times she was the most beautiful thing I've ever set eyes upon, her textures so pure, her curves so precise. I sometimes did nothing but stand and stare at her. But at other times she wasn't that good."

"What did other men think of her?"

"Other men? Other men?" George almost shouted the words. "Most men who set eyes on her were frightened of her. Some were scared stiff. But a few, just a few, felt the same as me." George went on. "It was her moods you see. Sometimes she was so incredibly affectionate, so supremely kind that you felt totally overwhelmed. Humbled. But then she sometimes flared up, in a terrifying hostility that frightened everyone - even me."

"She sounds a bit primitive?"

"I suppose you could say that," pondered George, a faint smile creeping across his lips.

"Did you ever -

"Reach the Mountains of The Moon?" interrupted George loudly, pulling hard on his cigar.

"No. I did try to once though. But it didn't quite work out. One of her moods again. I was annoyed at the time but I got over it."

"By the way. What was her name?"

"Her name? You ask her name?" said George, a slight twinkle in his eye. "Ah yes! I forgot to tell you didn't I. Well she is called Africa."

READY FOR THE OFF.

Well, I suppose it was a snap decision made over thirty five years. However, as most people were not aware of its origins from years of poring over school geography books and leafing through stamp collections (mainly those of friends - I was not rich enough to collect in earnest myself) they could not be blamed for thinking that I had over-reacted to life's traumas of the past few years. The reality was that this was a culmination of a lifetime's subtle, but determined, plotting and planning. Some reliance on fate, but with a gentle nudge when the situation demanded. A positive step to turn misfortune into advantage, and the dream into an adventure.

The world is really just one big adventure playground. A theme park to outshine Alton Towers, and even Disneyland. The busy and noisy Far East, the vast continent of Australia and the sun (and rain) kissed islands of the South Pacific.

I know it is going to be good.

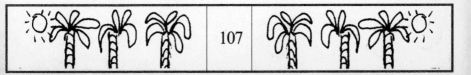

CHICKEN POX IN KOUKOU'S NEST.

The doctor gave me a pitying look;

"Go home, Signorina. Your holiday is lost." I phoned the airport. All the planes were full.

"I have to go home" I stammered "I've got chicken-pox."

"Mamma Mia!" said the travel agent "You can't fly with a contagious disease."

On the expenses of my insurance company, I booked myself into a hotel.

"It could have been worse." I thought as I touched the satin sheets.

But my life in luxury didn't last long.

"This is not a hospital!" They said as they pushed me out on the pavement with my two suitcases.

I took a taxi to the closest hospital.

"Haven't you got somewhere else to go?" Asked an angry nurse

"You should stay home in your own bed for such a tiny disease."

"I have no bed." I mumbled " I'm on holiday."

I had to cry before a doctor finally pitied me.

He was so beautiful that for a moment I forgot to scratch myself. I smiled at him, but he looked away in aversion and brought me back to the tragic reality that I was ugly -looking with all my spots and not in a state to flirt.

We went up an elevator and came to a corridor. Some old people with empty eyes lolled around in their pyjamas. One lady sang a lullaby, she seemed to be completely in her own world.

"God!" I thought. They have put me in the department of senile patients. Here I am less likely to contaminate someone with a child-disease.

A door opened. Five people came out, crying loudly. "MAMMA!" they yelled. A quick glance into the roon made me understand. She laid there, about five metres from me. Her spirit must have been flying above us that moment, on its way to heaven.

The doctor left me in a tiny room with pale blue walls.

Ten minutes later he came back.

"I have something here." He said and gave me a little white pill.

"It will stop the chicken-pox from itching and make you feel better."

And Boy! Did it make me feel better! I floated on clouds and decided to do some sight-seeing!

"Ciao!" I said to the lullaby-singing lady. She smiled to me with a tooth-less mouth.

I took the stairs down, and was suddenly surrounded by babies, screaming wildly behind glass-walls.

I remembered my illness and panicked, aware of the danger I had put the new-borns in.

"Lord Forgive me! Don't let the babies be ill." He must have heard me, because all of a sudden I found myself in front of a door with a painted cross.

I went in quietly.

All around sat people in their dressing-gowns. They sang, accompanied by the priest on guitar. The only lyric they repeated was "ALLELUIA".

"Here I am on holiday," I thought "instead of visiting the Vatican, I'm having a pyjama-party in a church."

I took the elevator up. I felt dizzy.

"Where have you been?" A hippopotamus-looking woman took my arm and led me into my room.

"You are supposed to stay here!" She said as she closed the door. I could almost hear the prison key.

I slept for nineteen hours. My head felt heavy and I was hungry.

"Is there any food for me?" I begged a nurse.

She came back with a packet of milk;

"Buon appetito!"

I drank it directly from the packet. I didn't have a glass.

Take my advice! If you want to lose weight - go to an Italian hospital!

I tried to sneak away to the hospital shop. But...

"Where are you going?" There she was again, my own private spy, the hippopotamus woman. "You must stay in your room."

Behind that rough edge, she had a heart of gold, as she did my shopping.

After five days a skeleton thin doctor came into my room. He was so skinny that he must have been fed only by hospital food.

"You are not contagious any more. You may leave."

"Thank you." I stammered.

"Make sure you do something with your hair." He commanded " You look like a witch. Una strega!"

He put a cigar into his mouth and went away.

The beautiful doctor came to help me with my luggage.

"I heard that you are from Sweden" He said smilingly "What are you going to do here in Rome?"

"Look around." I answered.

"I know some nice places I could show you. Do you like to ride vespa?"

I laughed, happy that my Roman holiday could finally begin.

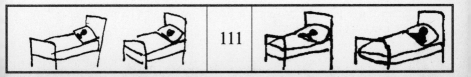

LUNCH IN ARUSHA.

The New Arusha Hotel has a grand entrance and khaki clad personal safari guides by sleek land cruisers awaiting their high fee clients. We passed the doorman with some trepidation. Were we going to be turfed out by some flunky or clerk? No. So far so good.

We looked through plate glass windows into expensive curio shops, where American and Japanese tourists purchased carved ebony Trees of Life and high quality Batik at high prices. We had a wash in the spotless conveniences and we marvelled at the 'proper loos' (we were by now used to squatting and the long drop facilities).

Having investigated the cafe, we decided that perhaps we should lunch there rather than the restaurant, but we were approached by a portly gentlemen in immaculate morning dress, who suggested we should follow him to the buffet. Without arguing we walked along a corridor overlooking the well-laid-out tea garden and on to the large and grand restaurant.

The Maitre d'Hotel led us grandly to a central table covered in a snow-white cloth and gleaming cutlery. Four waiters materialised to hold chairs and flap serviettes over our laps - laps which bore filth from our travels. Not even a haughty glance from the staff! Menus were passed to each diner and we were left to consider our choice. A glance around showed the 'fading glory', the wall-paper was a bit scruffy and the carpet a bit worn.

The wine waiter approached and took our order for Safari beers and bottled water. The head waiter approached and hovered explaining that the menu was fixed - a hot buffet - and would we like to start with the soup.

The other diners were a group of Americans with their private guide, a group of wealthy African women in exceptionally smart local costume and dripping in gold, and an African family with very well behaved children. We felt tatty and out of place.

The soup was served by smart waiters wearing white gloves with their outfits and accompanied by fresh white rolls and creamy butter - something we hadn't seen for our whole trip. The hot buffet dishes contained many vegetables and there were a host of meats to try, some reasonably familiar and others definitely not. We filled our plates.

The sweet trolley contained all the local fruits, European cakes and gateaux, Tanzania coffee followed with 'After Eight' mints.

The meal over, we relaxed and waited for the bill which eventually appeared in a leather folder. We had all tried to guess the price per head and our suggestions ranged from ten pounds to eighteen.

I opened the folder; 6500 Tanzanian shillings each including drinks - six pounds fifty!!!

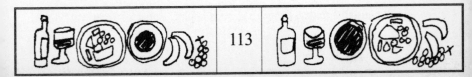

FIRST DAY BLUES.

The man smiled, baring teeth stained red with Betel juice. "Greetings to you my most esteemed friends", he said.

"Get lost" said Wink.

"That is a most unfortunate start to our relationship" replied the man. "Please to let me introduce myself"', he continued "I am Gomez. I am your ear cleaner."

"I will show you" he said, producing a much thumbed notebook from beneath his shabby robes. "I am coming very much recommended to you".

Gomez handed me the grubby little book. "Read here please." He said.

I flicked through the pages reading glowing testaments to Gomez and his ear cleaning prowess.

One read: 'Gomez really is the business. One session with him and my Walkman has never sounded better! Give the bloke a chance!' Greg - Queensland Australia.

I turned to Wink. "Is this guy for real?"

"I don't know" replied my friend, "but it could be a bit of a laugh. Come on let's give it a go."

Gomez needed no encouragement and magically produced a small tobacco tin that he opened to produce a variety of instruments. He sat himself by Wink's side and inserted a pair of long tweezers into his ear. After a little fiddling he pulled out a large piece of ear wax which he placed on Wink's knee.

"You see my friend, how is it possible to hear the birds sing with such dirt in your ears?"

Within a few minutes Gomez had dug a small pile of debris from Wink's ears. Now it was my turn. Gomez went to work enthusiastically and before long a mass of wax appeared from the depths of my lug holes.

"There is one more operation to perform before my employment is finished." Said Gomez. With a flourish he produced a glass full of brown liquid from beneath his turban.

"What's that?" I asked warily.

"This is ear medicine." He replied, and despite our protestations he proceeded to pour a measure of the liquid into our ears. The 'medicine' fizzed and popped alarmingly as it went in.

"There" he said with a chuckle, "you will now be able to hear perfectly the nagging of your wives!"

"Here, you can have ten rupees", I said handing him a grubby note.

Gomez grabbed the money and, with a conjurer's skill, made it disappear into the depths of his robe.

"Many thanks to you my friend", he said as he packed away the tools of his trade. He shook our hands and melted into the crowds.

A well-dressed elderly man had been standing nearby watching the proceedings with great interest. He approached shaking his head, making small tutting noises through his teeth.

"You are very foolish to have done this thing with this man." He said.

"What do you mean?" Wink asked warily.

"This is a bad man." He replied. "Do you know from where comes the fluid that he is putting into your ears?"

"No."' I said, sheepishly. "What is it?"

'This man, he is getting this fluid from the batteries of old cars.

"What!" I shouted, jumping up. "He's put bloody battery acid in our ears! We're going to go deaf!"

"You must come with me immediately," said the man. "My brother is a pharmacist, he will help you."

Lamely we followed the man as he took us back through the streets of old Delhi. We found the pharmacy down a busy back street where our friend talked to his brother. Before long our ears had been filled with drops and stuffed with wads of cotton wool.

"This medicine is very expensive", said the old man handing us a bill. "You must be paying my brother four hundred rupees."

"Four hundred rupees!" I gasped. "That's twenty quid!"

"Yes my friend," replied the old man, "but it is a small amount to pay to avoid deafness."

I couldn't really argue with this logic and reluctantly handed the money over. I looked across at Wink.

"We've only been here six hours," he said, shaking his head sadly. "We've already had acid poured in our ears and been ripped off for twenty quid. How the hell are we going to survive the next six months?!"

THE LIVING TRAIN.

There were bodies everywhere. Bundles huddled around piles of luggage. We were tempted to bed down with them, but our train was due. So instead we sat on our packs, and watched the blanket heaps rise and go about their morning ablutions. Soon the track was an open air bathroom. People were cleaning their teeth and squatting backwards over the rails, and all respectfully staring straight ahead. Meanwhile beggar children ran around charming people for money, and the rag pickers resolutely continued their way up and down the line.

No one queues in India, and as the Vasco - Hospit train pulled in, the platform moved as one towards the carriage doors. People seemed to have everything they owned with them - huge trunks and bundles of firewood. The only exception was a drunk man. He was carried in and deposited into the luggage rack with only a bottle of coconut fenney (the Goan equivalent of schnapps), tobacco leaf cigarettes, and the clothes he must have been wearing for at least a week.

Being on a train in India is rather like attending a family party. There are children everywhere and lots of good food, and very soon the prevailing politeness dissolves into noisy discussions and disagreements. Like everyone else, the family opposite us had brought tin pots of dahl, rice, and soggy popadoms, and offered to share. However, after our unfortunate breakfast of 'chum chum' (sticky green balls of marzipan), we felt it more sociable to decline! Instead we communicated with mute nods and smiles, while young men spat red clots of pan onto the floor and hung precariously out of the carriage.

Then the luggage rack man finished his fenney and started looking for trouble. Those below him had tolerated the occasional intrusion of limbs and bidi ash, but when he dropped his empty bottle down onto a young woman their patience snapped. He was hauled down, bones clattering against the iron rack, and ejected from the train, where he met with the long bamboo sticks of two delighted looking policemen.

Life in the carriage settled back to sticky, cramped normality. Babies howled and lush scenery crawled past the iron bars of the windows. Beggars hauled themselves up and down the aisle, some carrying cards which explained their 'dead parents and dumb relatives.' Everyone looked away, and handed them a few coins. At every station food sellers jumped on with baskets of samosas and peanuts (in India even the starving are never far from food), and glasses of sweet milky tea appeared through the windows, heralded by nasal chants of 'chai chai chai'.

Some people drifted into heat induced slumber, while others chatted idly or watched the young shoe-shiner blow huge smoke rings. Everyone was hot and no one had enough room, but by now we were numb to it and didn't protest. Just like everyone else, all over India!

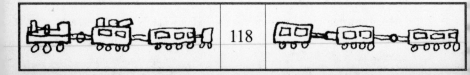

EGYPTIAN MUMMY.

Upon stepping out of the plane in Egypt, the first thing to hit me was the heat! I love hot weather, and my, was it hot!

The journey to the hotel was absolutely amazing: I stared out of the window from the coach and felt that we hadn't stepped out of a plane, but a Tardis. It seemed as if we had travelled back in time - the dusty roads, the attire of the locals, donkeys, chickens and goats strutting across the road 'willy nilly'.

Our hotel room overlooked the Nile. There was a huge cruise liner moored at the bay in front of the hotel and by complete contrast on the far side of the river there were mud huts where people still obviously lived. They carried water in large pots; half clad, dirty children played on the river bank; this coupled with the opulence of the cruise liner, appeared completely bizarre.

On the last day of our holiday it was my birthday and we had the most fantastic meal in one of the restaurants on the complex. The waiters found out it was my birthday and bought a crepe suzette to the table still alight and all gathered around singing Happy Birthday. When we had finished our meal we strolled down the banks of the Nile - the air was really warm, the gardens were a mass of exotic flowers and fauna and in the black of the night was a multitude of stars. As we stood there I felt sure we would never forget Egypt.

How right I was!!! We went to Egypt on the 8th June 1993 - and on the 8th March 1994 our son Joseph Luke Parkinson was born - well we had to call him something biblical and I didn't think he would want to grow up with the name Pharaoh.

No, I shall never be allowed to forget Egypt.... After all I went there and came back a mummy!!

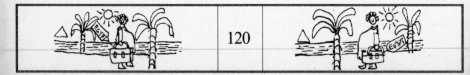

THE HAMMAM HOUSE OF HORRORS.

The guide book stated that: "a Hammam is not only civilisation at its most refined, it's also a bargain at around one dollar". It was neither!

Visions beckoned of steamy rooms of white marble and strong-fingered masseurs rubbing fragrant oils into my bronzed back.

I found the not unpleasant looking building (with a not-so-pleasant looking old man outside) and asked my friend to meet me in an hour. He was "shooed" away by three women who gathered around me as I tried to ask for a massage. They smiled blankly. Eventually one woman, whom I guessed was in charge because she was shouting the most, nodded and led me into a dingy room with a filthy bed and a dusty floor. We were followed by the old man, his son and the other women. They stared at me in concentrated concern as they produced some brown solids from a tin, miming rubbing motions. This was not turning out the way I had imagined..

One of the women led me by the wrist down cold stone steps into a warm, dark, dank underground concrete cavern that was swimming in water that gushed in rivulets and gurgled down huge drains in the middle of the floor. Down one side were open concrete booths that reminded me in both appearance and heady sweet smell of the cow shed we had at home.

Water was running everywhere. The booths were alive with semi-naked women of all body shapes, concentrating on bathing and scrubbing each other. Some were seated, others standing but they worked in pairs rubbing and scrubbing each other and washing one anothers' hair. Their bodies, usually well concealed below long robes, appeared doughy and lumpen. The sight of their pendulous sagging breasts and dingy underwear did not prevent me from noticing that each pair of eyes looked my way with at least suspicion, if not a little hostility.

I was shown to a filthy bed and given a pair of well-used 'flip-flops', at least three sizes too small, so I went barefoot: Contracting a veruka or athlete's foot seemed the least of my worries because the woman began undressing too! I shook my head "No!" I shouted, "I want massage!"

She managed a smile which revealed a single rotten tooth, then pointed to me to undress. I sat in my underwear and wondered what I had let myself in for. She filled a large galvanised bucket with hot water and unceremoniously flung it over me then proceeded to rub me down with a vigour more usually reserved for a Cheltenham Gold Cup winner!

"Ouch! That's sore!" - She was using a loofah with the subtlety of a pan scrub. More water was chucked over my head with no warning and I was lucky not to loose a contact lens! I was not so lucky when she was washing my hair because an earring came out on impact and "sloshed" down the giant drain.

The boss lady appeared with the tin of unidentifiable brown stuff and before I could say "excrement!" she was rubbing it over me. It burned and stung like chilli pepper, so I stopped her before she got into the nooks and crannies. Was this the massage or a Tunisian version of soap and shampoo?

My mind ran riot as I no longer merely wondered if I was going to get my massage, but whether I was ever going to get out of this torture chamber. I began to worry about the money in my 'bum-bag', which I'd handed to the woman upstairs for safe-keeping. "Maybe they'll drug me and rob me or perhaps steal my clothes" I thought.   My new travel companion was the only person who knew I was there, and we weren't on sufficiently intimate terms for me to meet him wearing only my knickers!

"Enough of this nonsense," I thought to myself, "you've tried the 'going native' bit and admit it, you're uncomfortable. Just forget about the massage and get yourself out of here as fast as you can". So mustering as much dignity as I could, I stood up, walked towards the door and demanded my clothes. Pulling them on (there was no towel), I stumbled up the stairs into the sunlight. My friend was waiting.

"Wow! What a great massage I had! How was yours?"

DODGING THE MILE HIGH CLUB.

I arrived at JFK happily exhausted and longing to complete the last leg of the summer and sleep a whole week in the same bed.

Once on the aircraft, I settled into my seat. The man squeezed in tight next to me turned out to be an American gospel singer which could have been interesting, but wasn't!! There are people who, while they cannot sustain a conversation, cannot let go with dignity - and this was such a man! I spied a row of four seats in front to my left with no-one but a small Japanese business type occupying the far seat. I explained I would prefer more leg room and quickly shifted before he could argue.

Safely ensconced in my new, spacious accommodation I began to relax - tipping my seat back, only to be greeted by squawks of irate disbelief from the gentleman behind who explained that it was impossible for me to recline my chair as he was a traveller with special needs.

I closed my eyes, and prepared to wake up to a London dawn - but the thoughtful gospel singer stretched over to inform me that they were showing "Beauty and The Beast" (aptly enough!) for the in-flight entertainment. I smiled wanly, thanked him and set about sleeping again. I had paid little attention to my new neighbour save to ask him whether the seat was taken, though I felt that perhaps he understood my needs when he woke me for the drinks trolley circuit - a nice, cool, creamy glass of Baileys was just what I needed for the perfect night's sleep.

It was when I turned to curl up and sleep for the last time that the real trouble began. My kindly neighbour proffered his hand in what I presumed to be a good-night handshake - and in the spirit of travelling camaraderie I took it. After what seemed like a long pause, it became apparent that he had no intention of releasing my hand and a cloud of doubt scudded across my mind, but I decided that perhaps he was merely an innocent reaching out across the gulf of loneliness that comes from travelling alone and decided to leave my hand where it was. A few moments later my doubts were revived as my neighbour leapt across the divide and placed his spare hand on my thigh. I realised something had to be done and calmly removed both his hands from my person without opening my eyes. Not to be discouraged, my neighbour confidently leant his head on my sleeping shoulder. This could not be ignored; opening my eyes, I grunted rattily and moved away. Still, international body language was not being understood and my pursuer grabbed my hand insistently, thrust his face at me, and implored me to teach him how the English kiss. This caught me somewhat off-guard and the only reply I could think of was, "sorry, I really don't feel like it at the moment." This clearly wasn't strong enough and it took another half an hour of shuffling, snuggling and staring before my neighbour finally lost interest in me and plugged his headset into the film.

At seven a.m. English time we arrived in London. I stood, exhausted, to take leave of my tormentors. My amorous Japanese neighbour appeared refreshed from his sleep as he moved forward to rejoin his tidy wife, seated three rows in front and the Gospel singer huffed past with a disdainful sneer, on to bigger and better things.

I hauled my dirty self off the plane and onto the tube - for once relieved that nobody looked up.

MISSED FLIGHT.

It's a strange affliction, punctuality. I am extraordinarily punctual, I can leave my house two hours late and arrive at my destination an hour early. I am always early for the bus or the train and I don't know how I do it. This punctuality, however, does not extend to the catching of aeroplanes.

I know you're supposed to check in at least two hours early. I know you're supposed to wait in the lounge and keep a tab on your departure time. I know you're supposed to do these things, but I just can't seem to do them.

I have been given a thick ear by a stewardess for being the absolute last person to board an aircraft bound for Canada, for delaying everyone on board yet arriving with a 'what, who, me?' expression. I have even been wheeled through security, drunk as a lord, and perched on top of a luggage trolley pushed towards the departing plane. But I think the worst case of flight delay happened to me the first time I visited Turkey.

I had been there for about a week, staying in an idyllic, almost undiscovered paradise called Akkum. It had been my first foray to this country and I had taken it to see a mate - Howard - who was living in a tent on Akkum beach and hindering the waiters and staff of a nearby fish restaurant. He'd been there for about six months. I was to be there for 10 days.

Life in Akkum was slow, languid, warm and hassle-free. In fact it was so without problems that even decision-making became an ability beyond my reach: should I go for a swim, or stay on the beach? Should I eat dinner or wait until dinner came to me? Should I stand on a stool when hanging my trunks out to dry, or stand on tip-toe?

I got up one morning and went for my usual hangover-curing swim, but couldn't shake the feeling that there was something I had to do. This was strange because I was on holiday, where the thing to do was. . . nothing. Lots of it. I didn't even have to buy anything: I was all stocked up on sun-tan lotion, my toothpaste hadn't run out and my pictures had been developed at the little photo booth at the top of the beach. Still, I couldn't shake the feeling that something was amiss. I even told Howard about it and he couldn't think of anything either.

It finally hit me around four o'clock in the evening. I was supposed to have caught my flight home at eleven that morning. I had totally missed my flight. My parents were waiting to meet me at the airport.

I phoned home and got an ear-bashing. They seemed to think I had done it for purely selfish reasons, wanting to extend an idyllic holiday. That was all well and good, I said, but had they realised that I was now stuck in Turkey with no money and no way of getting home? That quietened them down a bit.

My salvation came in the guise of Ahmed, the owner of the fish bar, who just shrugged his shoulders and said "no problem." Like, yeah, right.

He took me into town, a fishing-port place called Mersin and, from there, into a Turkish Airlines office. He waved my ticket at the man behind the counter. The man behind the counter turned and shrugged. A heated conversation in Turkish followed. I was gradually informed that firstly the ticket was void and that secondly, it wasn't their problem. Ah well, I thought, I am now a Turkish resident. However, Ahmed cunningly pointed out that I had no money, my visa would run out in one day and that, in short, I would become a burden on the Turkish community, all due to the uncaring attitude of Turkish Airlines.

I got my ticket for a flight three days later. I didn't miss it.

THE ONLY ROOM IN TOWN.

I was brought up to understand that 'nice girls' were never found in brothels. That's why I never told anyone.... until now.

It was past midnight when I staggered under the weight of my suitcase into Montreal's Greyhound bus depot. I'd been visiting relations in Connecticut and was on my way to stay with a friend in Quebec. I thought it was too late to telephone, so decided to book into a hotel.

The clerk in the depot tried not to show that he thought I was an idiot. Didn't I know that Montreal was holding its Cultural and International Exhibition. Didn't I know there wasn't a vacant room anywhere in the city.

"Can't you suggest <u>anywhere</u>?" I felt and obviously looked the picture of dejection.

"Well.... if you're that desperate..."

"I am."

He wrote an address down, and within minutes I was in a cab relishing the thought of bed and sleep.

It was only when I paid the cabbie and he'd driven off with a smirk on his face, that the penny dropped. I realised I was in a down-town red light district. My destination appeared to be a doorway sandwiched between a strip club and an all night pornographic cinema. A brilliantly lit sign flashed over the entrance - 'Open Twenty Four Hours A Day'.

Oh well, I thought, I've nowhere else to go, so picking up my suitcase I went inside.

A greasy little man with a scar across his cheek sat at a desk at the end of the corridor. He eyed me up and down as I approached him, glancing at my suitcase.

"I'd like to take a room for the night."

He continued to stare and then turned to a board behind him on which were 'engaged' notices against the room numbers.

"Should be a room vacancy soon", he said looking again at my suitcase. "You expecting company."

I felt dreadful. What did he think I had in my bag, and why did he keep looking at me like that? Surely he didn't think....

"I just want the room to sleep in..... on my own."

He nodded, and I think he got the message but was obviously puzzled.

"You English?" He grinned, displaying a mouthful of gold teeth.

"Yes, and I hadn't booked accommodation in advance. That's why I'm here."

"OK honey, we'll fix you up. I'll get Shirl to boot out number six", he yelled into a back room and glanced again at the board. "They've just about had their time." He pulled up a chair. "Sit down and have a drink." A bottle of Bourbon and a glass appeared from under his desk. It was the last thing I wanted, but I felt too nervous to refuse.

When Shirl finally appeared, she was a dyed blonde with a cigarette dangling from her lips. A skin tight red satin dress stretched to tearing point across her ample bosom which cushioned several lengths of plastic beads.

Shirl gaped at me, obviously as intrigued in my presence as the proprietor. They held a hurried, whispered conversation while I attempted to drink my neat bourbon.

Eventually I was led up uncarpeted stairs to a dingy room that boasted a bed, a chest of drawers, a chair and an air conditioner that didn't work. A tatty curtain covered a window that wouldn't open and looked out onto a brick wall.

"Bathroom's down the corridor." Shirl flung a clean sheet at me, and departed.

I panicked when I found the key didn't turn in the lock. There was a row going on in the next room - a woman screaming obscenities, doors slamming and bursts of raucous laughter. Inch by inch I dragged the chest of drawers in front of the door. Then I realised I should have visited the lavatory.

I was too scared to venture out and bump into one of these characters, but nature had to be attended to. I used my thermos flask.

It was stiflingly hot, but I didn't get undressed. I lay my coat on the floor as I didn't fancy the bed, even with Shirl's clean sheet.

At dawn I was still awake. I crept out onto the street and found a telephone booth.

To say that my friend was surprised to be woken at that hour by a slightly neurotic woman was putting it mildly. There was a silence when I told him where I was.

"Are you crazy? Don't you know what that place is?"

"I do now."

He also thought me stupid, but I didn't care. It had made a change from the Holiday Inn, and how many other 'nice girls' have seen the inside of a whore house?

It wasn't until some days later when I was in the Ladies Room in a rather plush Montreal restaurant that I remembered - I'd left my thermos flask behind!

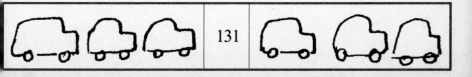

HELLO.

The kids in Shalu, Tibet seem to only know one word of English. It's Hello and they holler it all day long.

"HELLOHELLOHELLOHELLOHELLOHELLOHELLOHELLOHELLO HELLOHELLOHELLO..........."

I could carry on hundreds more times and even then it still wouldn't be half as irritating and deafening as the nuisance experienced when one is actually there. It's absolutely non-stop, completely maddening, and believe me an excellent way to annoy people. If you want to annoy someone start roaring "HELLOHELLOHELLO" as quickly and as loudly as possible to see how soon it is before you are choking and struggling to remove a pair of tightly clasped hands from about your neck. Not very long is it!?

They have tremendous vocal strength and stamina and excel themselves at pissing off foreigners by their 'hello' game. So, if anybody is planning to visit the beautiful Shalu Monastery and the village they will have a much more pleasant excursion if they wear ear plugs - ironically, deaf travellers say it is one of the most rewarding places to visit in Tibet!

A DOG - A RAT AND AN ELEPHANT.

The place was Bombay. The local time two thirty a.m.

I had arrived from London the previous evening on what was to be a holiday/business trip and being very tired after the flight decided to spend the night at a hotel near the airport before proceeding further.

I had been asleep for a couple of hours when I was awakened by what I can only describe as a 'nudging' at the back of my legs. Being only half awake I shouted "Get down Oliver -it's not morning yet" - (Oliver being my cairn terrier). But the nudging continued.

Now waking more fully I realised that I was in bed in Bombay - not in Barnes. It couldn't be Oliver.

I jumped up. A large rat jumped down.

I hit the bell-push hard and shouted so loudly that half-a-dozen hotel servants arrived at my room very quickly indeed. All shouting - gesticulating - and generally running around in circles.

A cricket bat was eventually produced and the rat chased into the bathroom where it was duly dispatched to the great warren in the sky.

They brought me a pot of tea and marvelled at what a lucky lady I was. Lucky?

Yes. One of the 'boys', a very wrinkled old man, explained in good English that according to the Hindu religion their 'God', Ganesh (the elephant god), has as his 'mount' a rat. Ganesh is the deity of prosperity that they invoke at the start of a new project so they believed he had come to my room, riding on his rat, to wish me a successful journey.

Fortunately I am not afraid of rats so could see the funny side of half a dozen men (aged nine to ninety) chasing round my bedroom in the middle of the night with a cricket bat followed by a discussion on an aspect of the Hindu religion.

The sequel to the story is that I had a very successful trip that finished in Madras and just as I was leaving the young lady who had been my guide, who knew nothing of this story, presented me with a little statue of - yes- Ganesh.

It sits on my dressing table and every time I look at it I remember the near-Whitehall-farce in my bedroom in Bombay.

BUNGEE JUMPER.

This jump was one small step for mankind, but a bloody massive one for Mr Mangat, perched on the edge of the Victoria Falls bridge between Zimbabwe and Zambia like a shivering sparrow. And this is despite the ninety two degree heat, and probably because I was letting all kinds of bizarre thoughts creep up from the side of my mind and mug the bit of my brain that wasn't yet a gibbering wreck.

Thoughts such as the best way to kill a mosquito in a small tent at three a.m. without decapitating your partner? Or the price of beer in north Zimbabwe, or whether or not my rucksack could be repaired and what was my brother's work address and who really shot JFK? All these and a hundred and one other thoughts joined together, only to die whimpering without answers as the edge of my personal time zone started to blur in with the increasingly scary real one.

"Don't luuk dowun maan" said the instructor from Natal in his routine - but - cheerful way. He counts down four - three - two - one - and then you jump. You jump because a mad part of you wants to; because the social part of you could never face the shame if you didn't and because you know your parents would rather you went to a forty eight hour rave with Psychos Anonymous in Amsterdam than do this.

They say your life flashes before you before you die, so that was the first sign I knew I was going to survive this. I did worry for a second that it HAD flashed before my eyes, but that it had been so boring that I hadn't noticed - this was shaken off to join all those other extinct thoughts and questions. There are really very few questions when you are diving towards a river that starts as a fingernail of green below you and then expands to a blue, brown, living water colour filling all of your vision. There is only a happy fear and the incredible imagination defying exhilaration that you are truly - madly - actually doing this.

The growing view of the underside of the metal bridge inspires some of the same feeling as you are pulled back by the cord, the existence of which, like the bills back home, you've temporally forgotten. In the gaps between the two extremes of space there is an unexpected second of weightlessness and a few more of silence, when you can hear neither the water nor the people above. Absolute silence seems to be rather more than the absence of noise, just like black is more than the lack of light. This makes one more thought join the queue; Simon and Garfunkel were right, there is a 'Sound of Silence'.

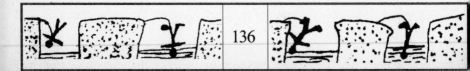

DEATH BONE.

When I told the waiter that a bone was stuck in my throat, he just smiled. "No problem mister, I get it out with a spoon." Moving too fast for me to resist, he produced an ice cream spoon with a very long handle, "now mister please to lift up your face!" I was glad to see him wiping it on his greasy purple jacket before ramming it past my tongue and down my throat. Several moments of rattling and peering later, he withdrew the spoon and shook his head "It is too much down mister, you must visit the doctor."

My girlfriend Susy took charge. With me gagging and frothing and the waiter flapping a torn bill behind us, she rushed us towards a taxi rank. Slumped in the back seat of the battered Mercedes I was having difficulty with my breathing and even more difficulty with the visions of what a Turkish hospital might be like. Our taxi driver pointed to a hill top where tower blocks shone. "It is the new Istanbul Hilton. You like to visit? Good price I have an uncle!" Susy just said very quietly, "we want to go to the American Hospital now!! No hotel, no carpet shop, no uncles. Otherwise my friend dies in the back of your car and you have to take him to the police station for free. You understand?"

The American Hospital was a clean modern building with no Americans in sight. The receptionist did not speak English. Susy warned her that I was going to suffocate in their waiting room if they didn't do something right now. The nurse explained that the throat specialist worked three streets away. We would have to walk.

We walked from the hospital to the consultant's office. Then we walked back to the hospital for an x-ray. Then back to the consultant, where he phoned the hospital to book an operating theatre. Then back to the hospital for me to go into the theatre. On the way we signed off all our travellers cheques to the various interested parties.

It was four in the afternoon by the time I was laid out on a trolley and wheeled into the theatre. The consultant said I was lucky, the bone had only stuck half way down my throat and probably could be removed through my mouth without having to cut open my neck!

I wasn't feeling particularly lucky. I had never had an operation before. A man came in and put a needle in my arm. He didn't speak English and so couldn't explain what was going on. I felt a numbness creep through my body. "So this is dying" I thought.

I came round from the anaesthetic when they shook me awake to sign a credit card bill for the operation. I could breathe. I could speak to Susy. We held hands and walked out of the hospital and into the sunshine and madness of Istanbul streets.

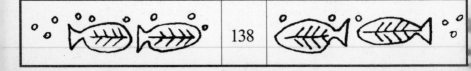

THE DEAL.

Mohammed announced it was time to meet the dealer. We assumed it would be a furtive meeting in a small back alley, a hurried exchange of money and merchandise; that is not the Moroccan way.

The pony and trap hailed by our host took us ever further away from the centre of the town. To my eyes, the area was poor, but without poverty. Mohammed was taking us to his home. He explained that, since his father's death, he was head of the household; he wanted his friends to meet his family. The house was a little larger than most in the immediate area; a low, two-storey sandstone terraced villa with a high wall and a large, brass-studded, wooden gate. As we entered Mohammed called out, within seconds the courtyard was filled with people. Mother, younger brothers and sisters, several aged aunts with their children and grandchildren, and a particularly fierce looking uncle whose face broke into a magnificent grin upon introduction. It transpired that those not of the immediate family had been especially summoned from their homes to greet us.

"It is time to eat," announced Mohammed. Our protestations were in vain. To have refused would have been as rude as our hosts would have deemed it not to have offered hospitality to guests. Led to a cloistered area at the edge of the courtyard, we were seated at a long, low table and offered bowls of rose-scented water to wash our hands. Mother, aunts and sisters brought dish after dish of steaming food. I can't remember all that we ate. I do know it was my first cous-cous, my first tagine, my first fresh figs. My strongest memory is of one of Mohammed's sisters. She was fifteen or sixteen, very shy and very beautiful. Around her head was wrapped a huge towel under which she had applied raw henna. Tiny rivulets of red ran down her cheeks and the nape of her neck. I think I was in love.

The dealer arrived not long after the meal commenced. From an ancient leather bag he produced a sheaf of marijuana, a solitary tobacco leaf, a large knife and a wooden board. His rhythmical, staccato chopping reduced the foliage to a large mound of kit. It reminded me of my father chopping mint to accompany the Sunday lamb.

All too soon the meal was finished, the deal was done and the farewells said.

That evening we sat on the terrace of the Hotel de France, sipping mint tea and watching the sun die on the Atlas mountains as life began in the square below. It had been a heavenly day.

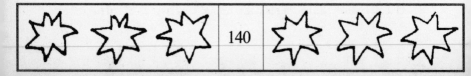

TOTAL ECLIPSE OF THE SUN.

The bus dropped us off on a dark mountain road and we hitched down into the valley to the small, sleepy Chilean village of Putre, which just happened to be smack bang on the centre-line of the eclipse's path, and was the designated place for everyone to meet up.

There were about thirty or forty of my friends there, and that night and the day before the eclipse we had an ecstatic reunion around a big campfire outside the village. The atmosphere was electric as people poured in from all corners of the globe. We partied all night, but at sunset on the magic day, one of my closest friends and I set off to celebrate the eclipse in quiet solitude together. Climbing to a high mountain top, we had a stupendous view of the valley below. Just the sun and the moon and the two of us!

We were up at about 12,000 feet, with a totally clear sky, in a place of outstanding beauty. I figured I was a bit of an 'old hand' at total eclipses (having seen one before), but I was in for a shock because this was no ordinary eclipse. As daylight faded and the totality began, three brilliant stars burst forth from the darkness - the planets Mercury, Venus and Jupiter.

They were sitting one on top of the other in almost perfect alignment with the sun and the moon, making a pathway of planets which appeared as a dotted line across the heavens. It was as if the Solar System's complex clock of planetary cycles had momentarily clicked into a state of perfect harmonious alignment and was chiming out across the Galaxy.

We both began shaking uncontrollably, and virtually everyone I spoke to afterwards said they had been shaking too.

Totality lasted exactly three minutes, but the jewel in the celestial crown was yet to come because, for me, the most earth-shattering part of this eclipse was the moment totality ended, and the first ray of sunlight shone through the valley on the moon and sped towards the Earth.

For a split second you could actually discern the path of this beam of light as it careered past the moon, and could see it APPROACHING the Earth across the gulf of space, at the speed of light.

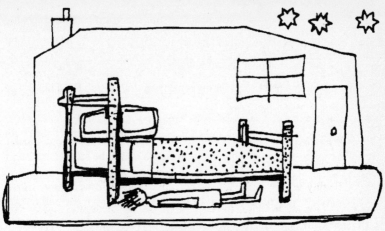

TRAVELS WITH MY GANGSTER.

Wedged between bed and hard floor, I decide that now is the perfect opportunity to consider believing in God. But would He take me seriously? And exactly how soon after my conversion could I start praying for him to save my life? I am in a tiny bungalow at 'Nick's', a hotel built amongst paddy fields on the popular island of Bali. It is approximately 4 o'clock in the morning and I am under the bed. Hiding. Curiosity may just be about to kill this independent traveller from Reading and I only came out for a holiday. The Indonesians are known for their hospitality and their desire to practise their English so I meet Sonny, a business man in a bar, miles from 'Nick's,' over a bowl of fried rice. Within an hour he has offered me a guided tour around 'his' island, a weekend shopping trip to Singapore, his Enya tape and more dinner. I succumb eventually.

Driving in his beautifully polished Landrover with air conditioning, an expensive German stereo system and blacked out windows, I wonder who on earth this man is. Usually when travelling I ask the questions and gather information. People enjoy telling me their life stories, their dreams, plans and even their bad jokes. But not this man. He takes me to sacred Buddhist temples and ugly dormant volcanoes, he finds me fruit bats and buys me endless dinners but he won't tell me what his business is. He offers to build me my own international school anywhere on this sunny island, which is pretty tempting when I consider my return to a slightly dull Reading. But he lets nothing slip about his personal life.

Finally he leaves me at a hotel watching dolphins from a beach with sand as soft as talcum powder but promises to return the following week. I go to bed contemplating this mysterious Indonesian who answers my questions with questions. Perhaps he's married? Or he's a mass murderer on the run? Or maybe he's from a strange religious sect and is in the process of converting me? He's probably a simple Balinese hairdresser who is enjoying my imagination.

The following day I'm whisked off to a 'Merdeka' fair in a nearby town by two locals. There are thousands of people and I become completely caught up in the Balinese dancing, the market stalls, the gamelan orchestras and the rickety fairground rides. Life is suddenly straightforward and clear again. People crack jokes I don't understand, introduce me to their families and answer all my questions. And just as I begin to breathe more easily, there he is in front of me whispering how he'd missed me. He's driven from one side of the island to the other just to make sure that I'd eaten. I swallow hard - especially when I realise he is not alone. A man stands slightly apart from him with his arms folded. Then it dawns on me I've been enjoying the hospitality of a gangster! Images of dead horses, cars being blown up and Al Pacino immediately fill my head. I am a little worried.

But as the weeks pass I almost become accustomed to the unexpected... the appearance of my gangster when I'm sitting at dinner with other travellers in a small non-descript restaurant... his offer of lifts when I fly in from other islands on flights I didn't know I was taking until the last minute.and the repeated guarantees of my safety while in 'his' country. His world is a world I know nothing of - a world of illegal dealings, murders, wads of money, mystery, danger, risks, and is therefore fascinating. And he is a man I will never really know - a man so desperately alone and lonely, who says he's prepared to turn his back on 'the family' and wash dishes if I'll marry him. But I can't and I won't.

So I shift uncomfortably under the bed, and wonder about the existence of God. In the early hours of the morning I have been woken up by feet pacing around the tiny bungalow. The gangster is long gone, having left me a silver bracelet and a promise to look me up in another life. The floor is hard and the bedsprings nearly rusted away, no doubt from other weary travellers sleeping on the bed.

Outside the pacing continues. Gangsters have enemies. Is it fair to ask God to grant me just one miracle despite getting myself into this extraordinary tangle? Probably not; pushing aside memories of *The Godfather* parts 1, 2 & 3, I squeeze my dust covered body from under the bed and walk carefully towards the window. It is important that I face one of the downsides of a gangster's life as well as the chauffeur driven cars. Having convinced myself that at any moment the door will be kicked in, the bungalow blown up and my head shot off with an AK 47, I take a deep breath and draw back the curtain consoling myself that at least I will die dramatically.

The pacing has stopped - a face stares back at me through the window but it is not the face of a hitman, it is the somewhat perplexed face of the hotel gardener! Perhaps God does exist.

ROAD TO GOA.

En route from Bombay to Goa, and I'm a captured audience of one - trapped on this bus for sixteen hours sitting next to Max. He sucks on an unlit roll-up cigarette and blows a cloud of imaginary smoke into the air. Have you ever noticed people like Max always tell you all the best places, all the good times and all the great people that were around ten years ago? I have this sneaky suspicion that if I had had the misfortune to ride in this bus ten or twenty years ago his conversation would have been exactly the same!

A black felt hat covers most of his head. Only his nose is exposed as the rest of his face is covered by a thick beard and a mop of long greasy hair, and he has worn sunglasses since he boarded the bus in Bombay, only removing them to examine the contents of a sandwich he bought when the bus pulled in for a toilet stop.

I try to concentrate all my thoughts on the long sun-tanned leg protruding from a pair of sun bleached Levi cut-offs stretched in the aisle in front of me. This perfect leg belongs to a five foot ten, blonde, blue eyed, all American student from New York. We had spoken briefly the night before, when she had been rummaging in her bag in the overhead luggage space, when a large jar, enough to moisturise the whole of India, fell out and hit me on the head. The pain was excruciating. She looked concerned "I'm a medical student, let me take a look". She gently parted my hair, professionally examining my skull for any future possible law suits. I was in love... she was also in love, but unfortunately not with me.

The journey continues and I spend a long time just gazing out of the window, a thousand framed portraits of Indian rural life, frozen for a moment in time and then lost forever to the speed of the bus. Each image has its own story, a tiny piece in a jigsaw of humanity that connects us all, the further you get from home the closer you get to it. The light begins to fade, shadows grow longer from the palm trees that line the edge of the paddy fields. Far off in the distance men are loading sacks and tools onto the back of a flat-back cart.

I think I know at that moment the reason I didn't fly down to Goa. Somehow I had become preoccupied with timetables, visas, passports and schedules. In the discomfort of getting there I had forgotten why I was travelling in the first place. The sun makes its daily exit, changing colour as it descends and finally becomes a ball of angry red as it slips behind the distant sky line. Soon the landscape has lost its colour and shape, now only a black backdrop to my reflection in the glass. I'm surprised to see it smiling back at me. Funny how happiness can sneak up on you when you are thinking about something else.

HEAVEN ON THE ROAD.

It's dark and I am deep in a forest. There are about forty strangers sitting under a tree. It's called the Banyon Tree. A Dutch man says that the tree has aphrodisiac properties. I can feel the power of its love right now. I'm in a dome with walls made with its roots and a ceiling of its leaves. You can see stars in spaces between.

Boom Shanka

What a noise everybody is making! Guitars, big drums, little drums, flutes, bells, shakers, clickers, voices, and one man on soprano saxophone. He tells me he has come from London, and is on his way to Japan - but like so many travellers I meet, he has been delayed in India.

India... it sucks you in and holds you there. Maybe it will turn you upside down and shake your soul.We have a fire, but it is a hot night. We don't wear much. The chillum keeps circling. "Come on, share your dreams" sings a Samson-type man from Turkey. The music's rising - manic drums - I am urged to my feet.

The next day. I don't know how long I slept or what time it is. An old man sits on a rock with a basket of breakfast. "Coconut cake, Honey cake" he repeats softly. People buy fruit and share. The fire dies, the sun rises. Birds chat, the people quiet. Meditative. Beautiful music on the boom box - ambient, classical, Indian vibes run together. "Drink coconut" says the old man, before picking up his basket, putting it on his head and climbing away - over the rocks into the forests of Arambol, North Goa.

I remembered a dream.

I was sitting on a rock

at the edge of the sea

when along came a human

who said to me,

"Life is like a cup of chai

it's sweet enough until

the day you die."

I dived into the sea

and swam out far

because Dolphins beckoned me.

Who are we to say

what is to be?

Look up to the clouds

and see life float

gracefully.

There's no rush!

It's the journey

that matters

in this reality.

WIND UP.

I've been around the world in 21 days, yet it takes just one supposedly straightforward trip into London to qualify for my own travellers tale from 'Hell'.

My wife and I were on a V.I.P. London weekend and arrangements had been made for a car to meet us from the train at King's Cross*. Apparently the driver was to be waiting for us, holding a nameboard to help us identify him. After some while we had still not made contact and after searching every conceivable exit, to no avail, we telephoned the hire car's office. They confirmed that their driver was indeed on the station's concourse, outside a well known stationers. On noticing a well dressed, gloved gentleman we approached him and thankfully he was indeed our chauffeur. He apologised on behalf of his company for keeping us waiting, adding that he'd thought this particular job had been a 'wind-up'. En-route to the hotel he continued - 'no dis-respect 'guv', but there was absolutely NO WAY that I was 'gonna' stand in King's Cross station holding a board with your name on." I suppose we could see the funny side later, after all our surname is HOOKER!

MOUNTAIN OF RICE.

I was already away from civilisation, but when the path eventually merged into rice terraces, I thought I had found Paradise. I stopped and looked ahead..... For miles all I could see were thousands of water-filled terraces, each with baby rice plants sprouting up like reeds. Each terrace was two metres high, so the prospect of falling into a watery terrace below, back-pack attached, was not pleasant. As I walked cautiously across these tight-ropes, I was put to shame by the few locals who breezed past me carrying immense sacks of rice and gas cylinders on their heads. Everyone I met smiled. The mountains were tranquil, and in this perfect climate I was at peace.

Finally I arrived in Batad, a beautiful village of twelve hundred people, which is surrounded by a site that is acknowledged as the eighth 'natural wonder' of the world - a steep amphitheatre of rice terraces: they are like giant steps to heaven. The residents here have none of the western world's desires or worries. They are unaware of television, since electricity cannot reach this pocket in the mountains. The only view they get of the outside world is of tourists. Thankfully there are still only a handful of us, due to the difficulty of access.

The children appear totally care-free, pigs roam the village steps and the families still live a traditional, slow-paced life. I stayed with a family for two nights and discovered remarkable hospitality. The aura of this peaceful spot was heavenly. But it is clear that life is a struggle for the locals - albeit without complaint. The road and forest are five miles away. They carry all their market-produce on foot over the rugged mountains, together with logs for firewood. Subsisting on their own rice crops is no longer enough, so many of the young are beginning to leave this 'paradise' to try and find work in neighbouring towns and cities.

In one of the village huts, I saw a woman (obviously one of the elders), who assumed a confident almost regal posture, wearing the unique signs of her tribe - patterned arm-length tattoos and a necklace of snake bones. She was initially reluctant for me to photograph her, but when a cheery eight-year-old arrived, and I played the fool with him, she relaxed. After I took the photo, the boy told me he lived only two minutes walk up the hill. "Would you like to come and see my family? My father is dead!" In some areas of the mountains, Catholics bury their relatives not in a cemetery, but in a separate grave next to their house, so I presumed he wanted to show off his father's gravestone. As we approached his house, I asked how long ago his father had died? The care-free boy answered, "oh, at nine o'clock!" I was stunned.

We suddenly arrived at his wooden hut, and I realised I had walked into a mine-field of embarrassment. Although the boy seemed cheerful, I was confronted with five family members, who were sombre, sobbing and wailing just outside the front door. The boy said "My father is inside sleeping". Dead people are considered to be sleeping until they are put in a coffin. I could see the boy's eagerness for me to go and see his father would not be shared by the other relatives. I declined to go inside, but offered condolences and asked them how it happened. Only six hours previously, the seemingly healthy father collapsed with a heart attack on his way down to his terrace. With the emotional and language barrier I was unable to say much of comfort, so excused myself.

Life is an accepted struggle for most villagers and although, for a passing tourist like myself, this simple lifestyle and awesome scenery seems like heaven, for the residents, simply living there can bring them a precarious step closer to reaching the real thing.

REDEFINING MISERY.

I was as red and wrinkly as a sun-dried tomato, and knew that before night-fall I would have killed either myself or the camel beneath me.

Raj - the camel - was not well, and I was not well either. As we ambled across the desert, Raj's swaying was like the rolling of a small boat on a large sea. He kept passing wind at regular intervals and he would suddenly stop and lie down - with scant regret for me! My own tummy-bug was having a similarly unfortunate effect, so we blew across the desert together in a fog of flatulence. My sense of humour, usually robust, became very fragile.

Something else contributed significantly to this journey from hell - my posterior, being of somewhat rotund nature, fitted the saddle very snugly. So snugly, in fact, that it was gradually being rubbed absolutely raw by Raj's erratic motion and each step was complete agony. I couldn't ever remember being so miserable - and there were another three days of this trip!

Finally Raj went one fling too many. "That's it - no more! I would rather walk than get on this camel again!"

It was seventy miles to Jaiselmer - walking was not the best choice for covering the burning desert! It took the leader thirty five minutes to convince me that it was not an option......and by which time I was feeling rather daft anyway. He heaved me up onto the saddle, and we set off after the others.

If things had been tough before, they were now beyond pain! The rope securing the saddle positioned itself under my raw bottom. The swaying gait ensured that this rubbed with exquisite agony that part of me which required no further rubbing. As I clung to the man in front of me - a position which normally I would have savoured - I simply hoped I was going to faint and have done with it. As I felt the blood trickling down my leg, I just prayed that the end of the world might come and end it all.

What seemed like centuries later, we reached a settlement with a tree. Spreading branches gave shade and the others were settling themselves for lunch. I prised my rope-shaped bottom off the saddle. Maybe there was a god after all. I pitched headlong onto the sand and lay there, my nether regions throbbing.

After lunch Raj and I were reunited. I was padded up so I looked like I was sitting on a cottage loaf! We took it slowly and the tents were already pitched when we reached the next campsite

Salve was applied and quantities of gin were consumed - and I was promised a lift on the supply wagon tomorrow! I limped to bed. The gin kicked in. I zipped the tent up as tight as a sealed packet of peanuts. I sank into my sleeping bag..... then I slept the sleep of a gin-soaked raw-bottomed camel rider!

NEPALESE HEAVEN.

Trekking through the Himalayas in January had been a truly incredible experience. The most spectacular scenery in the world, and a chance to view rural life away from motor transport, where Yaks and donkeys are the most reliable carriers of goods. Then there was the not inconsiderable fitness benefit that the whole experience had bought me... and then there was the cider! Now that was something special! At around twenty five thousand metres, the apple belt began and we were able to taste the local Scrumpy! - In addition to sampling a number of apple pies and crumbles of course.

We were about half an hour away from our guest house and still had five hundred metres to descend. To all intents and purposes we were drunk, having sampled much alcohol to celebrate each milestone. The only light we had on this freezing night was from the full moon which was slowly rising over the Annapurna Massif. We made our way along a narrow path, on the side of a deep ravine, in an increasingly erratic manner. To the right there was not much between us and the valley floor five hundred metres below. To the left, the snow-covered cliff rose steeply to the top of the ridge. As the moon rose higher I began to feel increasingly excited - almost exultant. I began to run. Turning back to face the way I had come I saw the most sublime sight that I will ever see. The shimmering light, from the disk in the sky, was almost dazzling as it reflected off the dominating snow-covered mountain range. In the centre of this were the dark, jagged shapes that make up the town of Jharkot, standing alone on its ridge. The sky was filled to the limit with every star in the universe and everything glowed silver. I could have sat there all night, but the temperature was dropping all the time.

We drunkenly ran the last section of the journey down to Kagbeni, in a ridiculously fool-hardy manner. Somehow we arrived safely. Once back in the comparative warmth of our guest house, we were able to celebrate the fact that we hadn't fallen to our deaths with a well deserved glass of cider. Now that was Heaven!

AFTER DISNEY.

We decided to head down to Orlando and Disney World. We booked into a Motel. Our room was on the second floor. It was already fairly late but the Disney magic was still in our heads and we could not sleep, so I went down to the local off-license for a crate of Miller Lager. We begin to drink. The conversation becomes stranger and we eventually stumble onto the subject of suicide. It is at this point that we suddenly hear three gunshots from the room directly above, some running and screaming and then two more shots. We scramble into the bathroom on our hands and knees. With the fear-of-death-feeling more apparent than is normal, I decide it is time to say a quick prayer. It was the kind of prayer where firstly you introduce yourself, because you know you haven't spoken for a while! After my attempt at a plea bargain, in which I basically agree to do anything that the Dear Lord deems reasonable, I crawl back into the main room and fulfil every childhood dream. I dial 911! Some woman tells me that the police are already on their way. Not feeling as comforted as I'd hope, I scramble back into the bathroom. We continue to sit in the dark for hours.

Spending the night in the bathroom is not what we had paid our money for, but we were glad to be alive! Assuming the situation is now stable, we go to the reception - the staff are what can only be described as evasive with any detail of the previous night's events.

Later that evening we came across a security guard who worked at the Motel. Although unwilling at first, he went on to explain how two men had followed some tourists into the room above us. They had watched them remove money from an ATM and then followed them back to the Motel. They then knocked down the door, stole the money and shot them dead!

The whole incident was really upsetting and I felt great remorse for the poor people in the room above us. However, part of me will always be thankful that the gunman got the right floor!

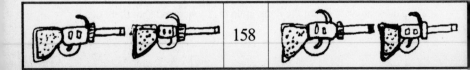

ON THE BUSES.

It had been the shortest journey in history. I was glad that I hadn't yet paid my fare, but there was little else to smile about. I was in Muang Khong, the principle village on Dhone Khong, an island in the Mekong river at the very south of Laos, on just the right side of the Cambodian border. More importantly though, I was on a bus and it was sinking!

I had boarded the colourful but dilapidated vehicle for a journey to Pakse. When it arrived at the ferry point for the first stage of its journey, I was pleased and surprised to find it half empty. This was highly unusual in this part of the world and I looked forward to an unexpectedly comfortable trip. I should add, however, that in Laos, comfort is a relative concept! This bus used to be a truck and had been converted for passengers by the addition of wooden planks for seats, as well as for a roof and walls. My bag stood on the roof along-side the usual vegetables and chickens in baskets and we descended the slope to the Mekong.

The ageing ferry was constructed of wooden boards laid across three boats: a Vietnam war era US pontoon either side of a motorised vessel and a slatted ramp on each side to allow access from the unpaved track. The driver began to edge the bus tentatively onto the boarding ramp. My next memory is of the ramp moving away from the bus, when it should have been moving under it.

And so it was. The ramp had collapsed and the bus was not boarding the ferry but pushing it away. Things then turned from bad to worse. For reasons best known to the driver (although to be fair to him he could have abandoned the vehicle by this stage), the bus ploughed into the river. The evacuated cabin was submerged in an instant, and the rest of the bus was fast falling victim to the river. The Mekong poured in through the open, and thankfully unbarred windows as fast as the passengers could throw themselves out of them. There was no hesitation, they seemed to know exactly what to do.

A Japanese couple, who had been sitting at the front of the bus, reacted like me - more slowly than the islanders. We found ourselves the last left onboard a now stationary bus, up to our waists in murky water and with no time to ponder our next step. The Mekong is not the sort of river in which the average traveller would immerse himself out of choice. The Japanese and the locals swam the short distance to the shore; my height allowed me to walk, the waters up to my shoulders and my valuables above my head.

We later re-boarded. The whole village looked on. People were in remarkable good humour whilst they fished their luggage out of the water. I felt slightly embarrassed to retrieve my bone-dry backpack from the roof, which had been the only part of the bus to stay above the water.

I asked the boatman if this happened often? "Not often", he told me in all seriousness. This was only the sixth time this year!

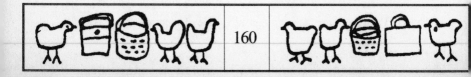

WHAT IS A TAXI DRIVER SUPPOSED TO LOOK LIKE?

To set the scene, I am a Brit, right down to my toenails - but circumstances beyond my control could not stop me being born in Canada, and thus I am entitled to a Canadian Passport.

My American godfather invited me to visit his family for the summer. The trip was fun. I then went to Canada to get a temporary job. Oh yes! I have almost forgotten the most important bit! During my travels in Colorado I had fallen and broken a number of teeth, which were slowly and painfully being put back by my Uncle's local dentist. My trip to Canada was a rest from the dental work as well as giving my godfather's family some space.

It was the end of my stay in Canada and time to go back for my final dental operation before going home to the UK.

The Greyhound bus stopped at the border. I began to wander what was going on when the border guard asked why I needed to travel to the USA for a dental operation. "Don't they have dentists in Canada?" He joked.

I explained. He then looked at my passport. "You don't even sound Canadian! So how did you get that passport?" Being born there was just not what he wanted to hear. I couldn't understand why he was making a deal out of this in the first place. However he now had a bee in his bonnet.

"How much money do you have on you?"

"Two hundred and fifty dollars" came my reply.

"How long are you going to stay?"

"One to two months" I replied ... Wrong again! He now had the ammunition he needed.

"You need to prove that you have at least twenty five dollars a day to stay in the USA. Sit down over there."

I started to realise that things were going pear shaped.

After a hour, a bearded man appeared at the desk. "I'm the taxi driver. I'm here to pick up the reject."

"You don't look like a taxi driver" said the official. I laughed inwardly, realising perhaps this guy had just got out of the wrong side of bed. But why was the taxi driver calling me a reject?

My passport was handed to the driver and I was escorted to the waiting cab. "Where am I going?" I asked.

"Back to Canada" said the guard. On the short trip back the driver told me that this sort of thing went on all the time and people like me were called rejects. I got my passport back on the Canadian side and was told that I was free to leave or do whatever I wanted.

I did eventually get over the border that night, but that is another story... Save to say the same border guard who had rejected me was forced to let me back to the USA and it was very satisfying seeing his discomfort at being overruled. Yes the operation was painful, but I did get what looked like my teeth back!

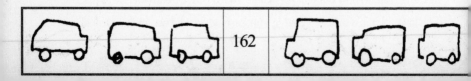

Daniel Gough

THE RIVER OF LIFE.

My name is River of Time

I am six hundred million years old

I come from Kenya

I live in the steep valleys and beautiful flats of Africa

My parents are the parents of all nature

I drink the fresh rain water

I eat the soil around me

I am a huge river, a river of life

I am going on the journey of time

My song is the song of nature

I have seen the dinosaurs and the Zulus

I have seen the life on earth.

BBE.

It stopped. Not a slow stop, but one that launched chewing-gums out of open mouths at dangerous speeds. I remember wondering as my fellow passengers' globules of gum went past my left eye, if their necks were all made of the same material - as theirs didn't seem to suffer from these regular halt jolts as mine did.

It was a few coffees past ten o'clock and the BBE (Belizian Bus Experience) was not even showing signs of yawning or getting ready for bed. Travelling in this converted American school bus carrying American missionaries and myself, it stopped where anyone wanted it to; whether to join it, leave it, or - nifty trick this - just do both at the same time while they discussed local gossip for five minutes at the edge of the road. It makes for a different approach to time, which I suppose is one of the reasons for travel - to step back from the rat race and join the human one for a while. Of course, there are other travellers who have an epic concept of time-watching, and my right ear was now hearing the joys of life after death from the convert to the 'Church of the latter day shock absorber Saints'; a man who managed not to sweat a drop, not even in the winner of the 'Most Humid Vehicle of the Year award 1997'.

Meanwhile the 1970's reggae music from the 1960's speaker was drumming notes into my other ear. This device is the most cunning in the masterpiece which is the BBE. Music seemed to calm everyone on these long journeys. The volume was controlled by the man (never a woman) with the open shirt and eyes at the wheel. His helper and partner in private road jokes, was usually a school leaver, waiting their turn to join the great central American knighthood of bus drivers. They seemed able to conduct news, rumours, grandmothers, chickens, or all four in huge treks across a region with a low literacy rate and a high curiosity level and to do this with style. No-one here would dream of putting up anything as vulgar as a sign. Here we remind people to give up seats to the elderly or infirm - on the BBE there are no such messages because it is automatic to do so, and if someone didn't the DJ/Driver/Porter would almost certainly make sure they did.

WHERE ARE THEY GOING?

Sitting on a train from Benaris to Dajeerling, India, clutching two Nikon cameras, two thousand dollars in travellers' cheques and a British passport, I was fully aware that I was a robber's juicy target. Furthermore, I wasn't thrilled to note that I was the only westerner on board and that there was an unidentified man carrying a rifle in the carriage. Curiously I asked another passenger who he was.

"He's a soldier, to protect passengers from bandits that stop the train by pulling the emergency cord and rob everyone," came the reassuring reply.

The next hour passed uneventfully and I relaxed. But just as my eyelids were beginning to droop the nightmare began. The train suddenly screeched to a halt and total panic set in. People started frantically grabbing their possessions and fleeing the train. Terrified and lost, convinced the bandits were coming, I had no idea what to do. Panic stricken, I looked round for the rifle-carrying soldier. He was nowhere to be seen. My options were none too tasty - either flee into the surrounding tiger-infested jungle or beg the bandits to spare my life.

By now the carriage was almost empty - just me and a couple of elderly men. In desperation, my gaze met that of the man opposite.

"Why are you looking so nervous?" he said. "Surely you're not travelling without a ticket?"

"Jesus," I thought, "we're about to be shot and all grandad cares about is having a ticket!"

The old man continued, "The government is cracking down on passengers without tickets by doing spot checks. As you can see, eighty of the passengers didn't have tickets."

The rest of my journey was truly blissful and my ticket never left my hand.

GORILLAS.

We have come to Kisoro, in the far south-west of Uganda, the last station before the Rwandese border. Half of the world's remaining big, black apes live in these mountains and very small groups of people are allowed into their sacred habitats. First there is a brief initiation ceremony in the park headquarters. We listen carefully as the rules are read out to us. No flash photography, no sudden moves, no sneezing as the gorillas can catch our germs, and if they charge, crouch and hope for the best. Lead by a tracker with a machete, a guide and a rifleman, we climb into the dense bamboo forest. For more than an hour we wait while the guide and tracker circle around searching for a lead among the many buffalo tracks.

Gorillas make a different nest every night, changing bedroom rather than sheets. A muffled cry comes from through the bush, the guide has found the remains of their last supper. There are droppings in an area with flattened vegetation and rings of leaves. Then, at the edge of a clearing, the big, dark primate, somehow awaiting our approach. A huge vaulted chest, solid centre, dressed in fur, his face, however, hairless and his cheeks shining like marble. In the branches behind there is movement and young ones are climbing up to see. A juvenile, perhaps a metre tall, is sitting on the path and looks at us with surprise. He walks back a few steps and lies down on his back, head on his arms, looking at us sideways in a manner so human. The atmosphere is surreal, and the boundaries of our species start to dissolve. Silverback stands, still chewing bamboo. He eats no creature larger than ants. The tracker is making low and throaty noises to put him at ease. He has been doing so for almost the full hour we are with them. Mother and infant are eating from a thistle, the latter tentatively stretching out, pulling a leaf from the stem and tasting it carefully. Then the mother suddenly charges. She rushes to us. Quickly we take two steps back, but crouching doesn't seem right, it would put us at eye level and might anger her further. The guide next to me firmly grips my arm. With our hearts still racing, we glance meekly at Silverback. But he is still calmly chewing bamboo.

The time has come to leave. This is their world and we belong elsewhere. We retrace our steps... and for many days to come the impressions linger.

GEOGRAPHIC VIRGINITY.

Graeme Watson made me an offer I could not refuse. Out of the blue, while having a quiet pint in Glasgow's West End he said, "I have bought a car for £50 and I am driving it to France on Thursday, are you coming?"

I felt the large finger of destiny point towards me. I was due a cheque in the post for some work I had done, and had no reason to say no.

It was the first time I had left the British Isles and my geographic virginity was broken with excitement and anticipation. We were soon in Dunkirk and soaking in the French resort. Early next day we headed for Paris, where we checked into a seedy hotel near the Gare du Nord.

The next day, we went our separate ways for a while. I did not know Paris and wanted to see the sights; walk along the banks of the Seine, see the Eiffel Tower, all the usual tourist stuff.

When I got back to the hotel, Graeme said he had been out with his bagpipes, busking in the French Metro. I was glad we had split!

That evening, we went to a fashionable district of the city, covered in restaurants that spilt on to the streets as people enjoyed the warm continental air. Graeme stepped out of the Metro in full Highland regalia: sporran, bagpipes, the lot - right down to the little dagger! I wanted to crawl into a hole. Once he got started, with the mega-decibels the pipes make, we would need more than that little dagger to get out of there alive, I thought. I was totally wrong! Loud it certainly was, but the French, whose taste is beyond anyone's ken, actually loved it.

From the first god-awful drone, they began to gather round until they were six deep in a circle around the mad Scotsman. Diners lifted their heads from their frogs legs and Bordeaux and listened intently, clapping enthusiastically at the end of each 'tune'. The entrepreneur in me began to see francs, and a way of prolonging my holiday!

With a nod from the master, I stepped forward, took Graeme's hat from his head and went round the gathered crowd asking: 'Un franc pour l'homme eccosais?' The return was incredible!

Not everyone appreciated the 'fine' sounds of the pipes. A cafe owner screamed at Graeme to move on but the crowd jeered and booed him and insisted on an encore. We toured the west of France: Orleans, Tours, Bordeaux, Biarritz, sleeping in fields under the moon; you could see the stars sparkle like Tiffany diamonds. We made enough to feed ourselves, a few drinks, and the petrol to get us to the next town. We never had to work hard. An hour a day at most, and we had the rest of the time to ourselves. You could hardly call it a working holiday. I only had to endure the groans and whines of the pipes!

We drove on to the Spanish Basque region, to Pamplona during the festival, and watched the running of the bull.

But there is more to the festival than the bulls. The town does not sleep for two weeks, except for a few hours at night when everyone gathers in the square and sleeps there. We were a natural part of the street party. The

Spanish were just as appreciative of the bagpipes as the French, and the going was just as good with pesetas as it had been with francs. I did not know the Spanish for 'Un franc pour l'homme eccosais,' so I stuck to the same line. It still worked, and we had bread, cheese and petrol for the car for the next day.

After Bilbao and San Sebastian and two weeks of bagpipe music, I decided I had had enough. I took a ferry from Santander to Plymouth and said my goodbyes to Graeme. He carried on for a further four weeks, making a killing in the French Riviera and Switzerland. I would not have thought it, but it was the most fun you could have with a car fit for the scrap yard, a set of bagpipes and a nutcase for a chauffeur!

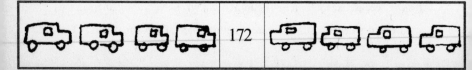

HIDDEN JEALOUSY.

She was tall and dark and all her children were handsome. Designer sunglasses perched on glossy brown locks. Her clothes were Armani. Her figure was perfection. This was not the Italian *mamma* of the movies.

"Maria!" she barked when I stumbled clumsily off the overnight Venice train, "take her bags." Her chic twelve-year-old daughter moved reluctantly forward.

"You're not like your photo," she sneered at me in greeting. I rather liked that photo. I'd been feeling good that day.

"Oh," I said.

"This is Pietro," she rasped. Her fat five-year-old son with the piggy eyes turned his back on me and snarled.

The car was hot, oppressive. I made polite conversation in broken Italian. Maria and Pietro bickered. She answered me in monosyllables.

Back at the house we met papa Federico and Mariluce. They were the blondes in this luscious family. Mariluce's hair reached her waist and her eyes were china blue.

We spent the rest of the summer at the beach house. My role was to cook, clean and look after the boy with the bulging eyes. He was the apple of her eye, the prize plant, the all important *maschio* of the family.

He did not like me. He did not like anyone. I told him to be a good boy, to do as he was told, to have a shower and eat his supper. He told me to go away. To go away, go away, va' via, va' via, go away, go away. We could not make it work, this five year old and I.

Maria and Mariluce grew browner and browner and happier. They liked Lido di Jesolo. Each day had its challenge. Each day there were outfits to select, boys to studiously ignore. Busy, busy, busy.

Their outfits all went back to the mansion to be laundered.

She told me to wash my outfits in the basin.

Maybe she was jealous. Maybe she wanted to travel the world. Maybe being young and beautiful and rich wasn't enough if you had three children and a plump husband. Did she resent my independence, my freedom to spend the summer looking after her son?

Maybe she was foul.

I was trying hard, I wanted it to be a success. I did my best with Pietro. I bleached the tiled floors of the beach house every morning without a murmur. I didn't chat much, but I was doing my damnedest to learn the language.

To her though, to that Italian woman, I was the English girl. I spoke nonsense. I couldn't handle a five year old. My carrot salad tasted of carrots (just carrots, *basta*). I was a weirdo with no emotions. I was a foreigner.

That was travelling hell.

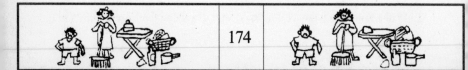

TRAVERSING TURKEY.

Old men wearing suit jackets over woollen vests and cardigans. A beanie with pompon over their heads. Faces of wrinkles and moustaches. Dressed for any occasion. Shopping, working or sitting in men's bars; stark rooms filled with vinyl tables and old men staring.

Women in cascades of black, only eyes free. Or women wearing green stockings, brown skirts, yellow jumpers and multicoloured scarves wound around their heads. Colour and fabric disguise the skin.

Wailing chants of Islam five times a day. The call to prayer over loud-speakers all over the country. Through the jumbled market streets, the chanting wafts, few stop.

Men linger in front of their shops, chatting with neighbours and luring tourists. "Where are you from?" is the question of every shop keeper. Nationality is used to define, compliment and attack. Bargain too much and you are labelled Scottish or Jewish; refuse to say "hello" and you are Russian. Mention Scandinavia and prices will dramatically rise. I would change nationality at whim, but everyone had a relative living in my adopted city.

Comments are hilariously funny, rarely threatening, but frequently sexual. "You are beautiful, I give you special price. Are you married? Do you want a Turkish boyfriend?" Or "What's cooking good looking, have I hassled you already today?"

One day we were ten minutes early for the opening of the Aya Sofya. A suited man asked us to look at his shop and have apple tea while we waited. Carpets hung from the walls, covered the floor and lay in stacks. We sat on rug covered sofas and discussed our travels. We drank apple tea and the seller drank plain tea, while young boys threw carpets in front of us. "What's the cheapest?" I said, staring at the tiny carpets. "I give you special student price of only US $200?" I really cannot afford that, but thank you for the tea" I stammered. "What's a good price for you?" he said as we stood. "I can make it cheaper" he yelled as we scuttled down the street.

We returned to our hostel one night to find the man from reception massaging a girl on my bed. She was ill and a pressure point massage was the key to recovery he reasoned. He offered me one too. He concentrated on the feet and legs placing pressure on specific points. He invited us to his house.

Disregarding common sense we said yes. We wanted to see a real Turkish house. Two stark rooms with peeling paint and no furniture. Cold. He gave us alcohol lotion for our hands, a sign of welcome in Turkey. "I will give you a massage" he said. "Take your socks and jeans off" he said. We decided feet only and then admired his book collection. "I want to leave" I whispered and my friend nodded. He said he would walk us home.

We also visited the house of a Turkish carpet seller. Carpets lined his floors and stuffed carpet cushions provided seating around a low table. He served barbecued fish and green chillies. He told us old carpets have souls and turned his music down at prayer time.

In the countryside a donkey trotted, carrying a man with a gun straddled across his back. Women with beaded scarves on their heads slowly led donkeys. The donkeys overflowed with loads of branches. Women in coloured skirts, long jumpers with white head scarves, shuffled through fields picking cotton and potatoes.

Cities are a mismatch of thrown-together buildings. Cascades of curves on mosques and square cement apartment blocks. Pavements with mysterious bumps and holes that drop into stairs.

We slept in caves, tree houses and garden sheds.

Getting off buses at bus stations we were seized upon. "Do you need a hotel?" people surround, enquire and begin the bidding. "How far is it? Does it have hot water? Can we get it cheaper?" we bargained. A man in Canakkale answered "if you do not like it you can kill me". He later told us the value of family in Turkey and how he wanted to marry and have children.

Early morning in Pamukkale we perused deserted restaurants for service. A lady limped towards us and whispered "Breakfast". She scuttled ahead through the streets. We trotted behind with our backpacks. She occasionally turned to ensure we were following. She opened a door and burst into a family room. Her daughter and five month old grandson were waking. They cleared the blankets and their beds became our seats. The grandson rolled around the couch playing with sheets, while the daughter cooked our breakfast and the mother went to buy bread. The daughter told us her husband died two months before her son's birth and showed us wedding photos.

Bus rides cross country with Turkish music screeching, a toy swinging from the roof bashing the windscreen with each hairy traffic move. On local buses people pass money for fares from passenger to passenger. The closest passenger to the front distributes the change.

Walking through castle ruins in Olympos, a teenage boy followed my friend and I at every move. I felt a hand clutch my bottom. I turned and screamed "Don't". I walked away and a hand squeezed again. I screamed "How dare you, you bastard". My friend chased him ready to punch, while I stood sobbing.

In a Turkish bath a lady took my hand and lead me to a room with taps spurting hot water. I was naked, she wore black lace pants. I sat by the tap and splashed hot water over my body. She lay me on a cement slab and lathered me with a soap massage and scrubbed until the loofah was black.

Wandering around streets we were given directions, offered jobs, boyfriends and accommodation. One man suggested US $8000 a month to be a nanny.

Despite the poverty of Turkey, beggars are few. At every bus station boys board buses, spinning silver trays stacked with cakes on their heads. Gold boxes with compartments for brown and black polish swing in young boys' hands. "Shoe shine" they scream. Boys flopping carpets in front of foreigners, delivering tea, chasing tourists down the street. "Can I help you spend your money today?"

THE 'GANNET' SURPRISE.

The Japanese are not noted for their relaxed laws, and the strict immigration procedures must be followed. In particular they have a rigid quarantine procedure, which is difficult to escape and violation of which carries heavy fines.

As we headed seawards the area was very crowded. We were outside the shipping lanes so luckily there were no encounters with larger merchant vessels. Most of the boats near us were fishermen, and we passed the occasional yacht arriving from further afield. As is customary, friendly greetings were exchanged from afar.

One boat seemed to be heading closer than the rest had done. It was aiming straight at us and was travelling at some speed, faster than our boat could ever move. This did not alarm me too much, since we could always get out of the way. 'Gannet' was quite manoeuvrable. But it kept coming towards us. When I was really getting worried it changed course and went alongside, to within about five feet. The yacht slowed down and the occupants seemed to be about to say something. I could see one of the crew holding what looked like a small cushion.

Suddenly he threw the object towards us. It landed with a thud in the cockpit and the boat sped away before we could say anything. The 'cushion' turned out to be a cat!! Alive and well after a journey through space, Graham, as he later came to be called, stood up, arched his back and promptly made himself at home by scuttling down below.

The owners must not have wanted the bother of going through quarantine and having to wait weeks for the cat's release. Rather than try and chase after them and cause ourselves delay, we adopted Graham as the sixth member of the crew and we enjoyed his company throughout the crossing.

THE SHINING PATH.

We were being held up by the Shining Path guerrillas. We all froze. Geraldine and I felt relieved now to have been harassed into sitting towards the back of the bus because we stood out a mile in our bright coloured T-shirts. We pulled a dark towel out of one of our bags to cover ourselves in a rather vain attempt to blend in. A kind man across the aisle was bemused by this and whispered to us not to worry. This kind of thing happened often and it wasn't true that they targeted foreigners. His thoughtfulness was reassuring in the few minutes of unbearable tension as we waited to see whether they would climb aboard the bus or demand that we all climb off. News reports of whole bus loads of people being shot in the Peruvian countryside raced through my head. I had never been sure whether these reports were true, but this wasn't the time to find out. Thankfully on this occasion the drama ended in anticlimax with the arrival of a small hat made of Llama wool which was passed between us for a contribution to the cause. Satisfied with their midnight fund-raiser, our captors then let us go.

We still had another six hours to go before arriving in Cuzco. Not knowing whether we would be attacked again further along the road made it hard to sleep. After a while, my attention was drawn to a woman who seemed particularly agitated and kept looking back in our direction. When I mentioned this to Geraldine, she told me that during the meal-break this woman had asked if it would be OK to store some of her belongings under our seat. Geraldine had agreed and thought nothing more of it. I began to feel uneasy. I put a hand beneath my seat to be met with the feel of cold metal in the shape of guns, covered over in some loose cloth. The reason for the agitation became clear as we promptly arrived at a checkpoint and armed police came on to search the bus. We showed them our passports and tried to behave as normally as possible, but now with images of being thrown into jail for gun running flashing through our minds. Happily we escaped that outcome as the search wasn't very thorough. We had to pass through two more police checkpoints and endure two more searches before arriving in Cuzco at five o'clock the next morning. We had collided with some of the clichés one hears about during the twelve hour bus journey, but also shared in the insecurity many Peruvians face on a daily basis. We didn't ask what the guns were for and would never know.

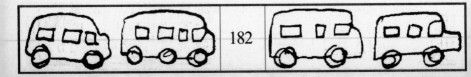

THE FLYING DUTCHMAN.

One afternoon in Kabul before the Russian war we were walking through a park when we saw a European coming towards us, tormented by a crowd of children at his heels. Without any greeting, he asked "Are you in a hotel?" repeating the question several times. After we replied that we were not, he explained. Apparently he had arrived in Kabul after dark the night before, tired (and probably stoned), and had fallen into a hotel picked at random. That morning he had issued forth eager to see Kabul, and had forgotten to check the name of the hotel, which now he could not remember! He was doomed to wander up one street and down the next in a nightmare, hoping to see something he could recognise. This was certainly the Rolls Royce of getting lost - when you did not even know what you were looking for - and a warning to us all!

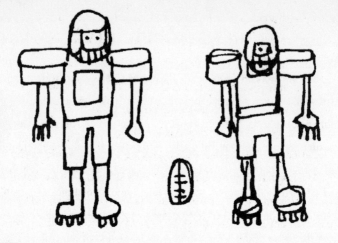

AMERICAN COLLEGE FOOTBALL HEAVIES.

American Football was a great love of mine at the time. It ranked only marginally behind the number one on the list of 'Jon's Great Passions' - my 17 year old girlfriend Caroline. I was 19, and cocky with it. "Been there, done that" trotted off my lips at regular intervals... but in reality I knew next to nothing.

I'd somehow convinced my beloved's parents to allow me to whisk her off on a fortnight's holiday to Florida, USA. I remember her dad who had done a years National Service almost thirty two years previously saying that "...a spot of 'R&R' would do us both the world of good." Why on earth anyone with a connection, no matter how limited, with the military has to constantly resort to stripping words down to their bare initials is way beyond me. Even more surprising perhaps, was the fact that he couldn't manage to grasp the two initials which were embedded in my mind.

So there we were, two young Brits abroad. The first week in Orlando sped by. All funfairs and life-size cartoon characters. Excellent fun ... but no football. Well that's not quite true. I managed to sneak a few late night glances at the cable channel in the hotel room. Interesting, enjoyable even, but no real atmosphere. Thankfully, the second week in Miami, home of the mighty Dolphins promised so much more. The thought of watching the likes of Dan Marino in the awe-inspiring Orange Bowl had me in a state of perpetual excitement for the previous seven days.

Bad news. The Dolphins were playing away. I couldn't believe it; despair, sulks and tantrums followed as I came to terms with the reality of an unfulfilled dream... which is when I saw the local paper folded neatly on the reception counter. Go Hurricanes! was the eye-catching headline. Fearing my luck had nose-dived permanently and that now we were to be subjected to some sort of Caribbean induced typhoon I took a closer look. Perhaps I wasn't jinxed after all. The Miami Hurricanes football team was playing hosts to Oklahoma in a crunch college game. What's more, the drama was to be played out in football's equivalent to St Paul's Cathedral - The Orange Bowl.

The following day. and two bus-changes later the pair of us were making our way through the throng in downtown Miami. The bus journeys had been particularly enlightening. The route had been lined with little grannies waving unsuspecting car drivers onto their front lawns promising them cheap parking - far cheaper than at the ground. Unfortunately at the end of the game, the same drivers would return to find a tribe of local gang members draped in various poses over their automobile scratching messages into the paintwork with some lethal looking mini-machetes. Only on payment of a large toll would they be allowed to leave - minus their hub caps of course.

In our conventional tourist gear of vest, shorts and a natty pair of flip-flops I guess we stood out a little from the crowd, the majority of which were decked out in the home teams colours. This included their faces, daubed a day-glow orange. Despite what I'd been led to believe back home by the footy coverage on Channel 4, the spectators were every bit as ferocious as their counterparts in English soccer. Several scuffles had only been prevented from escalating by a heavy police presence.

But thoughts of beating a hasty retreat were discounted when I saw the match day programme. Brian 'The Boz' Bosworth and Vinny Testerverde starred on opposing sides, and the hype surrounding them convinced me it was going to be a mammoth encounter. Both went on to earn fame and fortune in the big league, but on this day the laurels went to Vinny and his Hurricanes.

Sadly I am unable to give you any of the match facts. Our top price tickets had placed us in the centre of the hard-core 'canes' fans. Drugs and booze was flowing freely in the stands. A little too freely as it turned out. One half-cut Neanderthal decided it would be amusing to wash Caroline's hair in beer, and proceeded to tip the contents of his plastic glass over her petite unsuspecting head. In true Falklands spirit I was up on my feet as fast as a ferret on speed, subjecting the assailant to a mouthful of colourful and derogatory language.

With the last insult still passing my lips I became aware of the fact that he wasn't alone. In fact he was surrounded by others all wearing his tribal colours. All of whom were beginning to move in our direction and none of them were smiling. Momentary thoughts of head-butting the beer-chucker and going down in a blaze of glory faded with each persistent tug on my vest by my soaking companion. So it was with heavy heart, and tightly clenched cheeks that we sprinted, not easy in a pair of flip-flops, out of the nearest exit.

Some years later and before Caroline was old enough to know better I persuaded her to marry me. We now have two beautiful young daughters of our own. It's still some years in the distance but I can imagine a time when some pimply-faced youth will come seeking permission to take one of my girls on holiday. But I'll tell you this for nothing, unless he can do 100 metres in a pair of flip-flops in under 10 seconds, he stands no chance!

I LOST MY HEART TO AFRICA.

I lost my heart to Africa,
The colours, cultures, land.
I forgot my life before this time
And everything I'd planned.

Such many beautiful birds and trees,
Animals wild and free.
My eyes were closed to these before
But now these things I see.

New friends have come and touched my life
With new ideas and views.
New thoughts have entered in my mind
And soon now I must choose.

The life I left was true and straight,
The same from day to day,
But now I want much more than this
And I must find a way.

I've stepped through places far and wide
But never yet before
Have I stopped to think so long and hard,
To open up the door.

I think that maybe I'll return
To the safety of my past
But how long before I crave once more
The new line that I've cast.

My dreams are filled of Africa
Of those still left behind.
My heart will always hold them dear,
So clear inside my mind.

HEAVENLY ALASKA.

Seated eight to a dingy, we were ready to leave. We drifted slowly away from the shore, past the mighty ice blue Mendan Hall glacier, and towards the river on the opposite side. Suddenly I felt very small and vulnerable, surrounded by towering mountains, dark pines and icy water. The shiver of cold turned into a thrill of excitement.

So absorbed in our wonderful surroundings, we were hardly aware of the distant rushing noise until it became a low roar. Rounding a bend, the cause of the noise was revealed. The previously gentle, rippling river was transformed into a churning torrent. This was it!

Clinging to the sides of the raft for dear life, I braced myself for the inevitable onslaught. We were being tossed through the rocks like a piece of match-wood. The first wave to hit me in the face was the worst, especially as I happened to be screaming at the time and got a mouth full of icy water! It literally took my breath away. By now my feet were soaked. Every pitch of the dingy sent a fresh gush of water inside my boots until I was sure that if we capsized the weight of these would take me straight to the bottom.

In a rare moment when my eyes were open, I noticed a large rock in midstream and we seemed to be heading straight for it at great speed. Cries of warning arose from all the passengers as it seemed we could not avoid it. Then with a deft movement, the guide veered the dingy to the left and began to laugh.

"Gee I love that bit!"

We continued, alternatively screeching with fear and with laughter. I was really getting into this exhilarating experience when gradually, the rapids slowed down and we reached calm water once more. Swathes of moss hung from the trees and coated the rocky river bank. Above it all, the sky was the clearest blue I had ever seen. Nobody spoke. To break the peace of this magical place would have seemed sacrilegious. Only a solitary bird, unseen amongst the branches raised his voice in song.

Further on the river became less deep. Below us the water seethed with spawning salmon, so close that you could lean out and touch them. Many lay thrashing in the shadows, their mission completed, easy meat for hungry predators. It was here that the guide pointed out an eagle's nest high in a tree at the river bank. A solitary fledging perched on a nearby branch was waiting for his mother, who arrived on cue, grasping a huge salmon in her talons.

What a spectacle to end a wonderful day.

SEALIONS.

Whilst snorkelling in the Galapagos islands, I went in search of a family of sealions. I was lucky because I soon located them; one minute I seemed to be on my own, then whoosh, a group of youngsters appeared from nowhere and started to play hide and seek all around me. Then they were off, all except for one young pup who turned and seemed anxious to play - and the next twenty minutes were pure heaven. At last, instead of being chased I was quite happy to do the chasing and I spent ages stalking the little fellow who was playing with what looked like a piece of sea cucumber. He kept tossing it up and letting it go, always ducking and diving and catching it in his mouth and then he swam above me and dropped it right in front of me. It was so close that I could have reached out and let his toy fall into my open hand, but instead we both watched it float past me. He dived again, brushing right against me and caught it once more. We played this game for some time but as we drifted close to some rocks, he dropped it and it fell into a crevasse. Well, he was just like a kitten with a 'ping pong' ball that rolls under the sofa; he tried everything to prise it free, first with his snout, then with his flipper, all the time looking over at me as if to say "come on, give us a hand", but I had seen his teeth and declined. So like a kitten, he got bored because I wouldn't help him, and swam off to join his school friends, thereby ending an unforgettable close encounter.

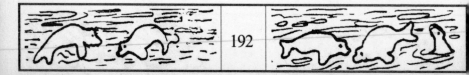

WET KINDNESS.

My girlfriend and I arrived in Western Samoa on Savai'i, in the heart of idyllic Polynesia. We knew no-one, had little idea of where we were going next, but it didn't worry us. We were free in this beautiful country without a care. For us it was times like this that made the back-packing life so enviously rewarding.

We decided to travel on a Samoan bus - obvious Westerners clambering onto a packed bus with huge rucksacks made us the focus of many curious eyes: and in a few minutes the polite questions started - these people however were not just passing the time of day - they were genuinely interested in our answer and were fascinated to discuss our life back in Europe.

I got talking to a guy sitting behind me, aged about thirty, he was dressed like the typical casual Samoan man in T-shirt, shorts, and spoke excellent English, frequently referring to his family and village.

We got off at an awe-inspiring expanse of dries lava that spread to the coast approximately two kilometres away. Perched about four hundred metres from the roadside was a semi-constructed wooden hut, consisting of a 'wonky' floor, roof and basic framework. On enquiring what this was, Joshua replied it was his Fale, and under the principal of 'Samoan Time' it was being gradually constructed. He said if we wanted to rest there then this wasn't a problem. Willingly we accepted and settled down for a siesta, not expecting to see him again.

Two hours later though, he returned with a friendly invitation to join his family for dinner - all fourteen of them. We were introduced to brothers, sisters, aunts, uncles and the parents who sat cross-legged in the family's eating-quarters with the pigs, chickens and ducks roaming freely amongst us and picking at the scraps. The food was outstanding - breadfruit with coconut cream, soup, fruit of all descriptions, bread, fresh fish caught that afternoon, followed by chicken and pork. We were treated like honoured guests, with a child sitting in front of us gently fanning the air. European King & Queen of Samoa? We definitely felt like it!

Outside, the storms that had been threatening all day were violently brewing up again. We thanked everyone and with the aid of Joshua's seemingly inbred night vision we headed back to our hut.

Joshua said we should stay with his family as the storms were looking fierce, but the uniqueness of staying a night in an open sided hut on a lave field was irresistible. As he left he handed us his eighteen inch machete, "just in case" he remarked "you never know, just keep it close to you!"

The strength of the storm was immense, and the accompanying gales were ripping through the hut. Outside, everything was pitch black. The power of the rain pounding on the tin roof was deafening.

Suddenly Antoinett nudged my side and pointed in the direction of the road. It was just possible to make out some figures approaching us, three or possibly four. The silhouettes were getting nearer. There were definitely four of them - and big guys too. I made a move for the machete under my back-pack. With the rain howling down, and the thunder booming, no-one would hear us even if we screamed our loudest. I had never used a machete before, and I didn't have any desire to start right now! We had both survived over a year of travelling and were due home in a couple of weeks. But this was serious. They were now about thirty metres away running and shouting at us. We had nowhere to hide. This is it, we thought. These four guys came right up to us, soaked to the skin. "We thought you may be getting wet out here so we brought you some polythene sheets for some walls". It was

Joshua and his brothers who, under the guidance of candle light, then got to work fastening the sheets to the framework.

We had never experienced a sense of relief and astonishment like it. This guy was incredible and would stop at nothing to ensure our comfort. We left Samoa with a great impression of this nations people: Caring, kind and extremely hospitable.

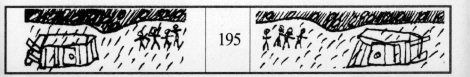

HEAVEN IS A LAKE NAMED DAL.

My ideas of heaven were vague until I spent two days in Lake Dal. It was not too safe to visit Srinagar, but we were told that because of landslides we could not return to Delhi via the original route, so to Srinagar we must go!

We arrived at nightfall. Awaiting us were a fleet of richly decorated Shikaras, the low boats with ornate canopies which would take us to our house-boats. I don't know what I had expected, but these were great wooden house-boats which had been built in the thirties by the British. Elegantly patterned awnings over the veranda, crystal chandeliers, a large carved dining room table with glass cabinet and sideboard, carpeted floors and bedrooms with en suite facilities. After five days of camping the luxury was almost unbearable!

It was bliss to sit all day on the veranda watching the world go by, though in many cases it stopped! Men alighted from the Shikaras and tried to sell papier-mache souvenirs, wonderfully embroidered shawls, ounces of saffron or exotic flowers. One man came selling home-made sweets. "Good day madam" he called up, "I am the delicious man!" And so the pressures of the journey slipped away. All I needed to do was watch the kingfishers flit by and observe the Shikaras trace a channel through the water lilies.

Over the Zojila Pass, which I could see from the boat, storm clouds gathered. There were no signs by day of the unrest swirling in the city, but by night I heard bangs. In the morning came reports of four bombs that had exploded during the night, but the lake remained tranquil and the vendors continued to sell their wares from boat to boat.

Some day I hope the situation there will be resolved and I will return, for this island was truly my idea of heaven.

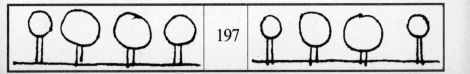

197

THE FACES OF HEAVEN AND HELL.

We started in 'Hell' and ended in 'Heaven'. Our tour took us to a former school that had been taken over by the Khmer Rouge for use as a detention and interrogation centre. At this stage we had no notion of what we were really visiting - the description we had been given did not even hint at the true meaning of the words 'Detention' and 'Interrogation' - although we were not so naive as to imagine it like a European prison.

The images of 'hell' began as soon as we looked inside the first room. The main impact on our western sensibilities was made by the manacles attached to the bed, the hooks and rings on the wall to which the manacles could also be attached. But it was really the row of photographs on the wall, the faces of the people who had inhabited this room only a few years ago that stunned us into silence. None of these people had survived, their stay here and the walls seemed to echo with their cries of hopelessness and despair.

All the other rooms in this block were the same and after a while the faces blurred into one composite image, an impression on our minds of innocence helplessly awaiting terror and death.

A final room was lined with more small photographs, more faces, rows and rows of them. The whole place seemed to have absorbed the groans and agonies of the victims, none of us had ever experienced a greater 'hell' - and the coach was silent as we drove away, each person with their own vision of the lost faces.

On the next day we took the short flight to 'heaven' - to see Siam Reap, a small town in the interior of Cambodia. As we approached what at first appeared to be crumbling spires of stone blocks, we gradually became aware of the feeling of being watched. Within a moment we could see stone faces emerging from the blur of the ruins of a temple. We were mesmerised, not by one face but by many, the survivors of the centuries of jungle invasion.

Most of the faces have crumbled to varying degrees over the centuries of jungle encroachment, but the few that remain intact must surely reflect a special sense of peace to anyone who sees them. Walking among the tumbled stones and climbing the remnant stairways to gaze at each surviving face was almost to approach 'heaven' and share it with them. Here one could sit and look at them for time without measure, perhaps waiting for the eyes to blink and awake, to pass on their knowledge of peace, their contact with divinity and that which we had been privileged to share for just a short time, their vision and taste of 'heaven'.

THE NUNS ARE COMING.

I was twenty. It was my first time in Rome. It was my first time abroad. In theory it was a college study-trip, in reality it was more a chance to soak up the atmosphere (and a little Lambrusco) of a foreign land. After three days, our group had already 'done' most of the usual tourist sites. At the end of a hard day's slog round the Vatican, I had struck out on my own and was wandering the streets with no direction in mind - just beguiled by the very novelty of it.

By now it was rush hour, the streets were noisy and fume-filled. As I walked along a line of nuns approached me. There were about ten of them. seemingly arranged in order of height. like a set of living Russian dolls - though not very living, the youngest looked to be about 70. As we came together on the pavement, the leader of the troupe (herd?... gaggle?.. what is the collective term for nuns?) held out her arm and spoke to me. Now, my Italian does not stretch much beyond 'Uno birra, per favore' so I had no idea what this wizened lady was trying to say.

I gave my best Gallic shrug.

Not satisfied with this, she merely repeated herself, this time a little more insistently.

'Sorry'...I' m English.. Inglese!' I said lamely.

Clearly, this was not what she considered a valid excuse because, stretching out her wrinkled arm, she gave me a short but firm shove towards the traffic. I could not understand what was going on. Seeing the look of bewilderment on my face she pushed me again, with much unintelligible gesticulation, till I had one foot off the pavement.

With the third shove I finally got the message - she wanted help in crossing the road. She wanted me, the archetypal innocent abroad, to walk into four lanes of Italian rush-hour traffic and somehow hold it back while the nuns crossed to the other side!

For a second, I considered doing a runner but the stony glare from this indomitable lady left me little choice - I had to give it a go. Like a captured bank robber, I stepped hesitantly down onto the tarmac and edged my way into the traffic with arms outstretched. Maybe it was the sheer incongruity of a lanky, tweed jacketed figure, bumbling amidst the speeding cars. Maybe the drivers were simply bewildered that anyone could be stupid enough to try such a thing - but it worked; the cars stopped. Like a modern-day Moses, I held back a sea of honking Fiats and buzzing Vespas. Irate drivers leaned on horns and hung out of car windows, gesturing madly, but still I held my ground. Even pedestrian crossings offer little immunity from Italian drivers, they merely weave round you; so, looking back, I suppose my 'miracle' had more to do with the presence of the nuns than anything I had done - running over a 'Lady of the Cross' must be a sure bet for eternal damnation.

Anyway, the nuns hobbled across the street and went on their way without so much as a 'Grazie'. As the last sandalled foot mounted the far pavement I raced for the sanctuary of the kerb and the traffic flowed once again. Even today, 15 years later, I still flinch if I see a nun coming towards me in the street.

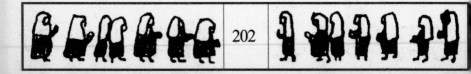

BOTTOM AND TOP ?

Travelling in Australia, we'd booked to go from Perth to Brisbane on the public bus service. Waiting for the bus to arrive to start the thirty-six-hour first leg, we overheard one of our fellow passengers say to his wife "I hope they've had that seat repaired". He went on to explain to us "We came over from Adelaide on holiday and my seat had got a fault - a spring had come through!" Painful. "And we've booked the same seats going back." The bus drew in and he saw it was the same bus, same seat, same spring. He demanded another seat but the driver said "We're fully bloody booked, mate, and we ain't got one." During what to him must have been long, long hours, the coach set down and picked up other passengers and he occupied the spare seats whenever they became available.

At Adelaide we left him still complaining, loudly demanding the name and address of the managing director of the bus company.

"If I don't get any satisfaction from him, I'll go to bloody Keating (the then Prime Minster) and if there's no joy out of him I'll take it bloody higher." We wondered who was higher than the Prime Minister. The Governor General? HM Queen Elizabeth the Second?

God?

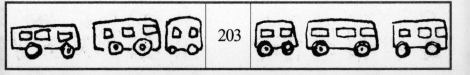

TEQUILA SUNRISE.

The man had gone by the time we left the water and we were totally alone. We might have been the only souls, sitting perched on the edge of the world. Night fell quickly so we lit a small fire to sleep round, preferring the open air to the cloying staleness of a tent. The flickering orange flames were the only light, save for the stars as we sat drinking it in. Darkness stretched away on all sides. Behind us the desert, silent, slumbering. In front the sea, reflecting the stars, and whispering hypnotically across the shore. A slight breeze pushed into the land, keeping the dust away and filling our senses with ocean. Through the gloom we could make out the bulk of the ship, silent in rest and atmospheric. Eventually talk gave way to drowsy dreaming. I lay back watching the stars, as clear as I have ever seen them, slowly moving along their celestial path. Occasionally there was the swift dashing dot of a satellite or the brief poignant blaze of dying debris burning in the heavens as it tried to make earth. As I was lulled into sleep by the rush of the waves I reflected that the dawn would not be long in coming, its grey light slowly warming our bones and pulling us from sleep, but that didn't matter, for under the stars, here and now I could feel almost part of the heavens. As I lay on what was surely the extremity of the earth, anticipating the dawn, I reflected on the primeval atmosphere of the place, inspired by the meeting of elements. My spirit rose high and I felt an embracing oneness with the universe, a oneness I knew would vanish with day-break, but yet would still live on.

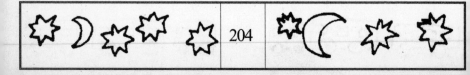

ONE ROUTE TO TIKAL.

On my National Geographic map the Peten region of Guatemala had seemed like an immense green mass cut out by an ancient god with a pair of golden scissors.

Tikal, probably the most impressive of the Mayan ruins lies in the heart of the Peten. At one stage up to two million people lived in the whole area. Today, about as many tourists visit the ruins every year - and with good reason.

By the time we realised that the route we had chosen wasn't going to be possible we'd gone too far. The back wheels of my bike were clogged with mud, stuck in trenches four feet deep. My friend's bike refused to move another inch. A mule would have been more co-operative. It started to rain. I was freezing cold and felt like crying. All of a sudden the trip's veneer of adventure was stripped bare, to leave a sodden pair of mud-caked idiots shivering under a tropical downpour, a long way from home.

After a consolatory sodden cigarette under a tree, we got on all fours and began excavating fistfuls of mud from my mudguard. After roughly half an hour of that, we managed to twist the bike around, and I set off back up the hill to find help. I pelted through the forest, going as fast as I could to avoid getting squelched all over again. I climbed the last brow of the hill and a clearing opened up ahead, but then closed again tightly ten metres on. I was going too fast. I panicked, and gripped the back brake.

Wrong move!

The back wheel slid out. I was thrown to one side, creating an arc of spray worthy of any downhill skier. Across the clearing's water soaked grass, I bum-slid, one hand still clinging to the brake and the other attempting to mop my face so I could see something.... but all I could see were the trees getting closer.

Man and machine came to a sticky halt a foot away from impalement!

I arrived in the village soaked through to the bones, and looking like a crusty who'd done one festival too many.

WEDDING AT CANA.

You cannot get much nearer to Heaven than being a special guest at an Arab wedding at Cana near Nazareth, the place where Jesus is said to have performed his first miracle, turning water to wine at a wedding. I was hoping for the same miracle, because the prospect of a Muslim wedding without alcohol did not exactly excite me. I met up with Assiz when I was working at a hotel in Tiberias, and he invited me to his cousin's wedding in Cana, a short distance away.

Cana has changed little since the time of Jesus. Arabs ride through its dusty streets on donkeys and the tranquillity is only broken by the sound of a rare motor car. The whole town seemed to have been invited to the wedding. The women were busy preparing the meal when we arrived. Several sheep had been killed and were being cooked on spits. Rice was being prepared in huge cooking pots in the basements of the houses.

"Are you a friend of Arabs?" The father of the bride groom asked. After being introduced to wedding guests I was given a cup of chai, and my arrival was announced on the public address system as "the special guest from abroad". Some tourists would have paid a fortune to have had this privilege. I had the freedom of the town that day, and any cafe I walked into gave me a drink on the house. I followed the wedding procession through the streets. It was headed by the bridegroom wearing a Kafia and sitting on a white Arab stallion. He puffed nervously on a cigarette. By his side walked a man who I assumed to be the best man and who was swinging a huge sword. Behind them came musicians playing eastern instruments. The wedding guests followed carrying all kinds of presents from shirts, to pots and pans, to baby clothes. The one notable absence was the bride, who was not allowed to take part because of the inferior status of Muslim women.

Eventually the bride did appear - with the bride groom and at the window of the house where they would live.

Guns were fired in celebration!

POORLY OVER PONGAL.

"Arrh Mr Allen, Vegetable Byriani," the doctor's words confirmed my suspicions but did little to relieve the situation. I have to admit that his perceptive nature was quite remarkable considering it was twenty four hours since my ill-fated meal.

It was our last night of a short break over the Pongal holiday and I was with two friends. The Vegetable Byriani had tasted a bit odd. But when I woke in the morning I felt fine. We started on our journey back and stopped in Quilon, further up the coast for lunch.

By this time, indigestion had crept in and I sat with a bottle of Mineral water, while my companions tucked into rice pancakes. Before they had finished, I decided to walk up the road to the nearest chemist for some indigestion tablets.

No relief though and I realised I needed a doctor. I had become feverish and disorientated.

At the local hospital, I outlined my symptoms to the receptionist. The room was already occupied by two German in-patients. We waited... and waited... and waited. Apparently there were no doctors available until after six p.m. How could a hospital not have a doctor present? It didn't make sense. We decided to explore and look for one ourselves, although normally walking through a maternity unit or a gynaecological unit would have made me blush, I was beyond caring.

Eventually I entered a room which turned out to be just around the corner from the reception, where we had originally come in. A friendly doctor ushered me up to his desk. The fever had developed and I was sweating buckets. I felt dizzy and disorientated but managed to explain my symptoms.

"A few minutes" he murmured after he had injected something into my arm, and he left me alone. I sat with my head resting on folded arms, and what happened was as much of a shock to him as it was to me. Regurgitated Vegetable Byriani all over the floor. I had no time to give warning or find a suitable receptacle. I started to recover quickly, but a sense of guilt surpressed a full recovery as I watched a young nurse put on a pair of gloves and grab a mop and a bottle of bleach.

After a ten minute lie down I was back to good health. I paid my forty pence hospital bill and continued on our journey. Needless to say we had missed our bus.

It was ironic that my Vegetable Byriani had caused so many problems over 'Pongal', the public holiday dedicated to rice harvesting. When we returned to the school where I had been teaching for the last two months I should have guessed what was about to be served up for our first dinner!

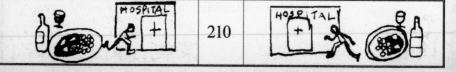

THE INCA TRAIN.

All through Peru, people had been raving about the ancient Inca site of Machu Pichu -its breath-taking scenery, the untouched landscape, the mystical auras, that sort of thing, but no-one mentioned the journey home!

By mid afternoon the station at Aguas Calientes was a mob of fleece jackets, back-packs, ethnic hats and over-priced cameras. When our train pulled in, the seats were full, the aisles were full, the steps were full! Any dignity, respect or love of local culture was lost in a flurry of knees, elbows and strategically swung rucksacks.

My friend, Graeme and I were already on one leg each when the fattest woman in the world calmly spread herself in the aisle and sat on our feet. I spent half an hour perched on my right leg, like a crippled flamingo, and another as Olga Korbut with my left leg contorted on an arm rest. Next, I was leaning at forty five degrees, balanced on a wizened old banana-merchant - my nose buried in his dirty embroidered waistcoat and my hand on the fat woman's round felt hat. Beautiful handicrafts they have here! Suddenly there was a shift of position, the fat woman twisted, the old man slid backwards, and I headed face down into a mass of feet, fag ends and orange-peel!

SAILING TO BYZANTIUM.

My eyes slowly opened to the golden flickering of the sun through my bamboo hut. I looked across the orange and turquoise rugs to see a huge ant crawl across my clock - 5.30 a.m., but I knew a beautiful journey lay ahead.

After haggling with the cab driver, we eventually set off through the mountains of Sinai. When we arrived at the bay, we clambered over the rocks and barbed wire, through dirty blackened trees and plants, goat skulls and fragmented flesh. Could a dolphin, the most divine creature of the sea, really have chosen this place as a home? Perhaps this was nature's balance, the 'yin' and 'yang'.

Staggeringly hot, the sun's rays beat down on the bay and then there it was....the first glimpse of the dolphin's fin; she was here and ready to greet Abdula. A deaf fisherman, Abdula had befriended the dolphin five years earlier while out fishing in the bay. Not so much Dr.Doolittle but Mowgli.

My adrenaline raced, but I felt very calm. Before I knew what was happening I was standing on a small blue power-boat, holding onto a thick rope for dear life. Sea breeze in my hair, sun on my back and salt water on my face. If this wasn't enough for the soul, the sun was blackened out of view, not by a cloud, but, to my amazement, by Abdula's soul-mate: She flew over our heads and plunged herself back into the ocean. We raced after her and her baby, the two soul carriers dipping, diving, turning, simply playing with the motions of the boat. The mother glided towards the boat, poked her head from the water and rubbed her nose against the wood. Abdula, in dulcet tone, murmured something to her and gave her a kiss; she smiled and replied. I was astounded - a man and a dolphin chatting.

Serenity fell, the boat stopped, the water returned to its blueness. This was it....time to immerse into the other world. I dived down with Abdulah and we embraced as if we were lovers and tapped each other on the shoulder gently, a kind of call to the dolphins. Usually I would have been quite nervous getting this close to a stranger, but it didn't feel that way; when two soul-mates come together to greet each another it doesn't feel strange. I looked down at the golden sand shimmering in the sun and there they were...the two beauties entangled in each other. They swam gracefully up to us and I reached out and stroked the baby; to my surprise he felt exactly like I imagined he would do. The mother swam around us - checking me out and coming close. As if she was human, I reached out my arms and we hugged belly to belly, I stroked her head and then she collected her child, brushed past our backs and glided off to the ocean bed. I felt I was home. Maybe I am from Atlantis!

All too soon we were back on the boat and speeding across the ocean to the shore, my face with a smile which could not be chiselled off! With tears of joy I hugged Abdulah, a stranger but an hour ago. I felt like I'd been let into a secret. I had not only communicated with a dolphin, but shared my emotions: I felt my mind, body and soul had been cleansed and as if a ton of emotional baggage had been moved.

A spirit from another land had guided me into my own spirituality, which had become cloudy from living in the city. On the dolphin's back I've " sailed to Byzantium" and the greatest and most beautiful thing is, I'm still on earth's planet to tell the tale.

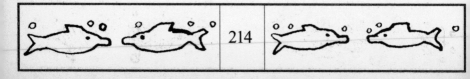

MALARIAL HEAVEN.

Malaria is a case of extremes! It's extremely unpleasant. Described as "a serious, acute, and chronic relapsing infection in man, characterised by periodic paroxysms of chills and fever, anaemia, splenomegaly and often fatal complications", its symptoms were not to be sneezed at. Its many names enchanted and frightened me, its history had made me in awe.

My parasites probably arrived in the fangs of an Ugandan mosquito. She was probably pregnant and wouldn't have buzzed as she completed her vampiric mission. The parasites which she didn't pass onto me would expand and kill her, but those which she did pass on faced an onslaught of my self defence system....gin and tonic.

And I got them in the end. They had given me some good hallucinations, including one where I believed I was a character in Paul Thoreau's 'The Mosquito Coast', trudging around in the jungle searching for ice. In return I gave them quinine, parmaqine, mefloquine, and just about every 'quine to kill them off, and so end their little journey. I don't bare a grudge against them, or the journey we took together. I wished them good luck, but hope they no longer rest in my Malarial Heaven!

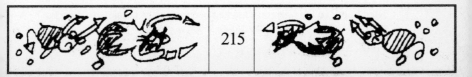

A DRIVERS TALE.

Ever been to New York? Ever been back? I've only been once - not that I don't like Big Apples but there is so much of America to see. Hopefully, I won't bump into another Raleigh. Bike - not Walter. Confusing? Alarming? It certainly was.

My first foreign driving experience: (at least any road rage I caused would be in English) I managed to persuade my wife that navigating through town would be easy - just keep heading north. Snail like, nose-to-tail hooting traffic on pot-holed Tarmac would be child's play compared to Hyde Park Corner at rush hour.

By the time we got to Fifth Avenue and 48th street we could almost smell clear mountain air. As we crossed the junction, a head down cyclist blurred into view from nowhere, clipped the front wing of my Chevrolet and capsized dramatically. Callous horns sounded as I went to help the poor man. But he was already on his feet and none too happy.

"You made a red there" he screamed. "You made a red. Where'd you get your driver's licence - from Woolworth's or what?" More horns. He gave them the finger. My passengers locked their doors. He seemed to be uninjured but I thought I'd better enquire as to his health. Try the English charm.

"No bones broken I hope."

"What?"

"Not hurt?"

He shouted to the gathering audience. "You hear that? Nearly f—g kills me then asks if I'm hurt. Jeez."

Then I noticed the bike, or what had been a bike, was scattered across the road in several pieces. A wheel here; a handlebar there; forks some yards from the saddle; pedals in the gutter.

He followed my gaze. "My bike's had it," he wept as he scrabbled together his trusty steed.

"I didn't realise you hit me that hard," I mused.

"Hey. Hey. Now let's get this straight. You - hit - me." He turned to the audience.

"He hit me right?" Some stared at the ground, others moved away. "This was a four hundred dollar cycle and you've totalled it." His finger was stabbing my chest.

The end came surprisingly quickly. Alone in the midst of blaring gridlocked traffic and a hostile crowd, the good old British phlegm disappeared. I pulled out our last hundred dollar bill intending to leave him details of Hotel Horrendous to which we would be returning. The biker snatched the note, gathered up his components and disappeared. The crowd melted away.

The headlight having been smashed in the conflict, we returned to the garage . Two hours later we were in a fresh car heading out of town once more.

White knuckles gripped the wheel. My wife gave stop-go instructions at each junction. The kids plugged into their Walkmans to block out the divorce-charged atmosphere.

As we stopped at 50th I sensed a bump from behind. My heart sank. As I got out, my friend from 48th street was storming towards me in blind anger as he screamed,

"You got no brake lights you idiot. And you stopped like you hit a brick wall. What the hell you doin'?"

I stood in silent disbelief.

"We met earlier," I offered.

Then he recognised me and his anger died "Jee-sus. Not again."

In silence he trudged to his bike, once more scattered to the four winds. He seemed strangely subdued as I helped gather the pieces.

Suddenly a voice barked from the footway. "Hey Coburn! Get that trash off the road and come here."

A cop was pushing through the spectators towards us. But Coburn was long gone and had left me holding the saddle.

"He bothering you?"

"We had an accident"

"No. You had a deliberate"

"Pardon?"

He began to reassemble the cycle. "You ever seen a circus clown on one of these. Rides okay till you flip the lever and. . ." The bike disassembled before my eyes.

The cop kicked the wreckage into the gutter as he reflected, "Good thing you never gave the jerk no money."

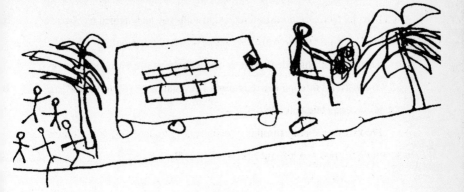

WEE OF THE NEVER NEVER.

We were imprisoned in Alice Springs by rains, the roads were like canals. Eventually, we put chicken wire over the windscreen to protect it from the stones flung up as our ancient Holden churned through mud. The road was a red river banked by bush.

We were on our way towards Ayers Rock, and sleeping in the car to save money. One morning we discovered that the car was totally bogged down. Laboriously, we lifted all our luggage, camping gear, water and petrol cans and spare equipment onto the only bit of dryish ground.

We still couldn't shift it, and we sat morosely waiting for inspiration to strike. My bladder struck first.

"You know," I said, "how when you're desperate for the loo and have to stop in the bush, a car always appears when there's no cover?" So I stepped bravely into the vast puddle and proceeded to do as nature intended.

No car engine greeted my micturition, but from the scrub emerged a troop of Aboriginals.

Mixed in age and gender, accompanied by camels and donkeys, they studied us for a while, then shifted the car with ease and helped us re-pack it.

Thanked with billy tea, plasters and eye drops, they wandered away and we continued through the red heart of Australia.

It was carpeted with flowers.

I had made the desert smile!

BODY CAVITY SEARCH.

I stuck my head out of the window and saw the border guards checking underneath the train for contraband people and goods. Eventually the train moved off again leaving Romania and stopping in no man's land while the whole process was re-initiated by the Hungarian border patrol. My bleary-eyed boyfriend joined me to watch the search as the guards tapped overhead ceiling panels and unearthed boxes of illegal goods.

We were ordered back to our carriage for passport control and were only mildly surprised when our passports were taken away for further inspection - it had become a common occurrence in Eastern Europe. They had still not been returned to us when the dog patrols came aboard to search the train. Again we were ordered into the compartment beside our Romanian co-passengers and told to identity our luggage. This done, we had to wait outside while the dogs did their business. Thankfully this was less messy than it sounds. Each of us then had to take our bag into the corridor while it was sniffed individually.

All the Romanian passengers were reunited with their luggage and seats while we were asked, politely, to leave the train. Being greatly disadvantaged by speaking no German or Hungarian, we had no idea why we were now being escorted along the platform by two armed guards and two dog handlers. Passengers hung from windows where we had once hung, and swung from doors shouting comments at us in aggressive tones and in indecipherable dialects.

I started to panic. What if one of our fellow compartmentees had been smuggling something - drugs?- and had hidden them in our bags while I slept outside in the corridor? A few days before, in Istanbul, we had heard of a traveller who was caught trying to smuggle two kilogrammes of heroin from Turkey to Greece by train. The dogs must have identified something. Why else had they pushed us off the train and kept our passports?

It did not serve as further comfort when the train chugged off into the darkness, Vienna bound, and we were left alone save for our captors and their dogs. They ushered us into the cell block and indicated that we should unpack our possessions, ready for inspection. I could hardly empty my rucksack quickly enough, desperate to discover what contraband had been concealed therein.

Containers were searched, shampoo and toothpaste squeezed out. Various soldiers and officials wandered in and out during the search, looking apologetic but sounding fierce and aggressive in their guttural tones. Nothing was found. Relieved, I watched in trepidation as they searched my boyfriend's bag. Still nothing.

I knew that it was now inevitable, but still shuddered at the snap of the surgical glove that indicated BODY CAVITY SEARCH. At least I knew that they wouldn't find anything in there.

Eventually an English-speaking soldier came on duty. Thanking us for our co-operation, he assured us that a train to Vienna would be along any minute now. We knew to translate that into meaning anything from a few hours to several days. As we hauled ass outside to sleep away the last hours of darkness on a track-side bench, I heard my boyfriend ask the guard what I had been too afraid to mention. Why had they searched us? "Oh, it's just routine", he replied. "The Austrian government require us to search any passengers on through trains who have been to Turkey. They get us to do their dirty work so that they keep their noses clean." He was tugged away by his sniffer dog, shrugging and wearing a rueful smile.

It was with great relief that we found ourselves pulling into Budapest hours later. We had decided to give Vienna a miss and made haste to the outdoor thermal baths for a soothing soak, massage and cold beer. So much for Western Civilisation.

A CHILDHOOD JOURNEY.

For as many years as I can remember I have always wanted to be somewhere overseas - clearly I am not a home-lover! My bedside is littered with travel articles - frequently read at night in the hope that I would dream of visiting an exotic location. At the age of eight I was invited into the life of a Nigerian Chief and his family in their ancestral homeland - Ijebu Ife. To get there meant passing swiftly through the bright lights and muggy atmosphere of Lagos - a capital city with vibrancy on a par with London and a crime-rate that dwarfs New York's. Despite this and the pot-holed roads, I made it!

Ijebu - a village brimming with people, animals, and smells - all so alien to me, and so appealing. Twenty four hour action - women cooking, children being beaten, men smoking and chatting, animals being slaughtered for feasts, and all set against the background of towering mosques which called the holy to prayer. As a child I felt no fear or danger.

The evenings were far more cultural - Nigerian society at play. Plump women in heavy cotton suits dancing with their men-folk. The stagnant smell of sweat failed to distance me - I joined in and was sprayed! There was a tradition of having money plastered onto the damp foreheads of the people while they danced. (The oil-boom meant the Naira was then a strong currency, but now you would return with a wad of worthless paper).It was fun and it made me feel positively rich!

Now all I want is to be rich enough to travel the world. I'm trying to figure out how to do it. Maybe I could become a travel journalist-what do you think?

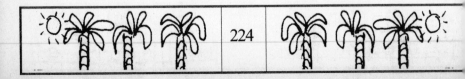

YOUNG TRAVELLERS.

The departure lounge echoes with the wailing and whining of small children and the screaming of babies. The three hour delay has done nothing to improve the mood of the Terrible-Two-Year-Old.

"NO. NO. NO. I don't WANT to go home!"

Max - proud father, and patience incarnate - gritted his teeth as the Terrible-Two-Year-Old squirmed and wriggled, pink with exertion in his arms. Five year old Patrick provided temporary distraction with his Darth Vader impersonation, and accidentally directed a flailing arm which touched the neat hairstyle of a boy of about nine who was sitting quietly by his mother. The boy looked up, shrieked "How dare you, you little creep." Leaping to his feet, he promptly caused a nosebleed. Mother smiled at her little warrior with an air of triumph; "I'm sure he didn't mean to hurt him", she murmured unconvincingly, as Patrick clutched the tissues to his nose.

"Ow, Gerroff", shrieked four year old Isabel to a new-found friend, who accidentally whacked her on the leg with a shinny red spade.

"Would all passengers awaiting the delayed flight TW165 to London, England, please make their way to Gate 23. This flight is now boarding. Trans World would like to apologise for any inconvenience this has caused."

We sigh with relief, scoop up bags and children and join the other passengers trailing wearily along the moving pavement.

The aeroplane was full to bursting. The no smoking lights went out. There was a chorus of clicking in the rows behind us. A cloud of acrid yellow smoke drifted overhead. I stood up, and starting rummaging in the compartments above our heads.

Pale faces loomed in the semi darkness. Dark Hair. Moustaches.

Headscarves. Shawls pulled tightly around children held on cramped knees. A cigarette held in every adult mouth. I frowned inadvertently, contemplating the next six and a half hours.

Children started demanding food. The steward informs me that as this is a night flight, people are expected to sleep, not eat - not until 5 am. We attempt to placate the children with left-over morsels of stale biscuits.

Patrick has just fallen asleep. Isabel has got it into her head that she can't possibly sleep in a seat, and is sprawling restlessly on the narrow floor space in front of our feet. Terrible-Almost-Two-Year Old, who has been distracted by the changing images on the TV screen, wails when it flickers and falls still.

The cabin is dark. All the children are now asleep. I have been dosing fitfully. My legs are completely numb. The pale orange sky is streaked with pink and yellow. Immense. Glowing. The sky had never achieved darkness on this journey, even at 2 am, over Greenland. We blink as the cabin lights come on, stomachs announcing their need for breakfast as we begin the decent towards terra firma.

HELL IS BEING TRAPPED ON A LAKE.

Visits from parents are always stressful times. Even more so when the visit lasts for a week and involves two younger siblings who need to be entertained with high adventure.

My folks had come out for a week holiday to Madrid where I was living at the time. Things had started off pretty shakily. I had only lived in the city for a few months and was unaware of all its delights, so I had inadvertently booked them into a hotel in the red light district! Secondly, every trip out had been marred by my remarkably poor choice of places to eat, where we were spending huge amounts of money - in fact most of the money my parents had saved by staying in what was ostensibly a brothel.

On the fourth day of their holiday I was overjoyed to look out of my bedroom window and see it was a fine day. Perhaps I was saved, and the holiday was saved! We would go to M&S and buy some sandwiches and then go to a huge park in the centre of the city.

Having polished off the snacks, we bought ice creams and really getting into the swing of things, my seventeen-year-old sister and I decided to go onto the boating lake - as a concession to our younger brother, who had already done a dozen things that were more appropriate for pensioners on a saga city break.

We got into the tiny boat and my parents settled themselves near the steps leading up to a statue of a past Royal on horseback. The park is notorious for pick-pockets, but my parents are clued-up individuals and were cradling their belongings in their laps.

What a shame that the same cannot be said for the two sunbathers sitting near them!

From our boat we had a clear view of them all and we noticed some doggy types circling the two sun bathers - a mother and boisterous toddler to distract them, while the others edged closer to their bags.

We frantically tried to signal to our parents but their senses were dulled by the so far disaster-free day, and they were blissfully unaware of what was going on a few yards away.

There was only one thing to do. "Oye" I shouted at the top of my voice, and in my finest Spanish I tried to tell them that their tickets home, passports, credit cards and pesetas were at that moment being stolen by the partners in crime of the adorable two year old that they were cooing over.

No response - from them at least, but the 'baddies' stood up and stared. In a moment of divine enlightenment, my parents realised what was happening. With lightning speed, I took the oars and rowed to the edge, praying my parents would be there to meet us at the shore.

God was looking kindly on us and we left the park by the nearest exit.

A successful day - and then back to the brothel!

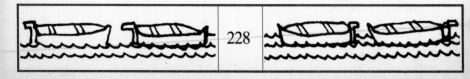

CHINESE BICYCLE TORTURE.

I hired a bicycle from the little shop outside my hostel with the few Yuan I had left in cash, so I could cycle to the Bank of China on the far side of the city. The friendly rental guy had wanted a deposit for his precious vehicle (bike thefts comprise most of the crime rate in China) and for this he wanted hard cash. On any other day this would have been fine but today just happened to be the day when I needed to change my US Dollars into local currency, hence my trip to the bank and the requiring of the bike. The irony of the situation was apparent, but just as I began to resign myself to the long wet walk, he pointed out that he also accepted passports as deposits. This is a common thing to do in hotels, both in Asia and Europe, to ensure that you pay your bill, but in this case I had my doubts. I had heard stories from fellow travellers of people locking their hired bikes up somewhere, only to find that they had gone when they returned to them later - the bikes having been liberated by their owner with a spare key! I was far less willing to risk my passport than cash in such a scam, but luckily I had my own lock and chain, so reluctantly handed the document over and headed off into the pouring rain.

I was pleased not to have been killed by the hoards of cyclists who, along with the drivers of the occasional motor vehicle, seem to choose to ignore any rules at junctions. However my good mood, which increased upon finding my bike where I had left it when returning from the bank, suddenly changed when I found it with 'added security'. I could not believe what I was seeing and it took me several useless tugs at the chain to fully accept the predicament. My first solution to the problem admittedly did not rank on the all time top ten of brilliant solutions! Noticing that the post was fixed into a concrete base, I wondered if I could carry the whole affair back to the hostel, and present it to the rental man to sort out.

Suddenly a man popped out from goodness knows where and began to make suggestions. After a lot of futile exchanged words and gestures, it gradually became clear that he was telling me to look for a man with a pointy hat. It dawned on me that this mysterious clue meant the ancient-looking policeman, who had begun to hover behind my new found friend. He was less willing than my friend to try and communicate. After what seemed like an eternity, it transpired I had been given my first ever parking ticket - the chain being the equivalent of a wheel clamp!

In the end I had no choice but to pay the fine, but not before learning a moral to this story which is not, as you might expect, never to let your passport out of your sight, but rather this: Never lock your bicycle to a handy post if the sign that it bears transpires to translate as "No Parking!"

RETURNING HOME.

I was born seventy years ago in Latvia, a small country by the Baltic Sea.

My house was by a river. There were about twenty houses in the street and where the houses ended a large forest of pine trees lined the bank. I lived there until I was seventeen years of age. Then the war and the Germans came. When they retreated, they sent me to Germany.

After the war I came to England and married an English girl and eventually came to live in Claverley, a small but beautiful Shropshire village. A lot of green fields and trees reminded me of home, especially in Spring when the blossom is out in the trees. But I did miss the river and the sea.

I decided to revisit Latvia, fifty years after having left. I wanted to show my wife my birthplace.

As the plane came in over the sea, I had a clear view of the river, the forest, my little village and even the bridge. When we landed, my friend's nephew was waiting for us with his car, and took us back to his house. He was married and had an eight-year-old boy. They were very kind and friendly.

The next day we decided to go to my old street, which was about four miles out of the city. This was not difficult, for buses and trams run frequently. I walked towards the street by the river. It seemed strange - there were no houses. My house had gone and so had all the others and the street was full of holes. Only the name of the street still stood in white letters on a blue enamel plate on a concrete post. I used to dream of going home, of talking to some neighbours - but now there is nothing, just emptiness and the sign I remember from boyhood.

In Claverley where I live, very little has changed. Church Street has not changed for two hundred years. I had dreamt that everything in my home village would be as I remembered it. I was very disappointed, but looking back, I am glad that I made the effort to go - it was certainly a holiday with a difference.

I WANT TO GO HOME.

I feel so ill, I swear my stomach is about to explode! Either that or my entire innards are about to fall out through my arse!

What am I doing here? This whole thing is just the most enormous mistake! I should be at home in the village pub, sitting next to a roaring log fire drinking mulled wine, as the snow banks up outside, not lying on this small, hard spiky camp-bed, wrapped in smelly woollen blankets with garish pictures of tigers on, in a horrible little room with the world's most feeble air-conditioning fan.

I should have realised that the idea of my actually getting to the Taj Mahal was doomed when we very nearly missed the train in Calcutta!

You would think that the end of the platform was the obvious place to wait. Unfortunately the train only went half-way down the very long curved platform, as we noticed when we walked along to investigate as the train started to leave, forcing us to try to sprint along the platform, beneath several backpacks and trailing trainers ,chains ,water bottles and dropping the best guide-book. Just managed to pull all three of us aboard, but as we were in the wrong carriage we had to sit in the only available space (in the corridor outside the gents) until we reached the next station three hours later.

Then we had an enormous argument with an entire family (father, mother, granny, five kids, three suitcases, four big string bags and several bizarre packages wrapped up in newspaper) who had our seats in carriage C, but then the guard came and pointed out that our tickets actually said carriage G! I feel really bad about that—I must learn to be less aggressive.

Next thing I know is I'm throwing up down a hole in the bottom of the train. Never before had I truly appreciated the term "projectile".

I am so cold. I hope the others get back soon (with tales of the breathtaking beauty of the Taj Mahal) and bring me some more blankets and water,...and maybe an orange...and possibly a pillow..and a huge double duvet...oh stop it!

Oh God! I cannot face another train journey!

Oh, my stomach! I'm going to have to face the dash down three flights of stairs, across the ground floor - and hope to God that there's no-one in the toilet again.

Oh God! I want to go home!

BANANA BOAT.

We spent a couple of days skipping from one island to the next, selling our bananas to a remarkable race of Indians known as the Cuna. After a few days at sea, our barmy little banana boat predictably ran into trouble. One of our crazy crew steered us smack into a shallow reef about two miles off shore, and we ground to a halt with a sudden crash.

We began wobbling on an outcrop of sharp coral and at the mercy of the waves. As each wave hit us we could hear and feel the bottom of the boat grinding against the seabed. Sooner or later it would grind a hole in the hull and then we would really be stuffed. As the urgency of the situation sunk in, all hell broke loose.

Everyone began shouting different orders and accusations at once! Panic gripped the drunken crew, and the only way forward seemed to be to unload all the cargo in the hope that we might be able to float off the reef, if we made the boat light enough. Bananas filled the air as all hands began to throw our precious cargo into the sea as fast as possible. It had taken twelve hours to load the bananas on board and now it was a race against time to unload them.

Hundreds of Cuna Indians, from three different nearby islands, had seen our dilemma and were coming at us from all angles in their tiny wooden canoes. Suddenly our stricken boat was surrounded by canoes full of colourful Cuna grasping at the air for flying bananas and fishing them out of the sea!

It must have seemed like manna from heaven for them to be getting this free food. They filled their canoes to bursting, then paddled home to unload and return for more. Some of them unwisely overloaded themselves and promptly began to sink amidst the madness.

By late afternoon every last banana had been unloaded and we eventually floated up and off the reef and were towed, helpless, to the nearest island by the Cuna. So there we were, stuck on a fairy tale desert island with no engine and no cargo, and my plans to reach Bolivia for the Equinox faded into a daydream.

YAK BUTTER TEA.

It's cold and dark. The sun is nowhere to be seen. It's morning but feels like the middle of the night. We jump onto the back of a lorry full of Tibetan people, who eye us warily. Suddenly, 'Mama' is there, pressing a full flask of hot Yak butter tea into our hands. It feels as if we are accepted, and so begins the trip to the gomba and the celebration of Buddha's birthday. It is the start of a memorable and special day.

'Mama' didn't join us at the gomba which was a shame since she was the person who told us about it. She ran 'Mama's Momo House' on the main road, a small dirt road in Gyanse, the third largest town in Tibet. She spoke no English or Chinese, only Tibetan, but she was good at sign language, which was the one language that hardly ever failed us. And she was the one who got us the lift on the lorry out to the gomba.

The stark sunlight bleaches the colours out of the arid Tibetan plane and hills which surround the monastery. It looks ruined at first glance, but then it comes to life as monks appear. Some wear their red robes and yellow hats, some dance in costumes and head-dresses, some carry long Tibetan horns. These are the pictures from 'Tintin In Tibet' and coffee table guide books, and now they have come to life and we are in the middle of it all. Around us are thousands and thousands of ornately dressed Tibetan people. There are no other westerners. A group of women invite me to sit down with them. Their hair is platted into enormous bejewelled semicircular head-dresses. They offer some celebration biscuits that taste like dry earth. I smile in appreciation. We nod and smile some more. Children surround us, staring curiously at me, with runny noses and dirt streaked faces. We are the side show and the bogey men to be scared of.

And the Yak butter tea? It was delicious, warm and nourishing - practically the only food we had all day. The monks took pity on us and as we watched the dances and ceremonies and gave us some of theirs as well.

The journey back on the lorry was cold, and it was dark by the time we arrived back at Mama Momo's house. We were welcomed as old friends and fed warm momo's and chang. We didn't want the day to end, and stayed talking until the early hours, but in the end there is only so much you can say in sign language!

Goodnight and Thank you, Mama.

MY FIRST MOTORBIKE LESSON.

Drip

Drip

Drip. Being from England I thought I knew about rain. I was wrong. This was RAIN. Imagine the strongest power shower you have ever seen, times it by ten, and then imagine that instead of coming out of a little nozzle, it's the whole sky. Well it was twice as bad as that!

The hut was on stilts and I had only just realised why. Through the cracks in the floor I could see a shimmering velvety pool of water rising towards me. Someone had built this hut in a pond. Where two days ago I had been sun bathing, a river had sprung up over night and a three foot deep valley to the sea had been carved.

The whole week was more of the same, and every night I was sung into insomnia by the multitude of frogs in the pond beneath my bed. The days were broken by the occasional trip up the beach - the tropical beach, in my 'wellies' and raincoat, to the small village slowly sinking into the mud.

After eight days my travelling companion and I agreed to leave the very next morning. The day dawned, and to our astonishment the sun came up with it. It was a glorious day. Rashly we decided to stay on and, to make the most of it, we hired a motorbike to tour the island. Neither of us had ever ridden a motorbike before, but the rain had obviously seeped into our brains as this did not seem to be a major obstacle.

Half a kilometre and twenty minutes later, two sheepish and mud en-crusted idiots gave up mud-wrestling the combustion engine. We realised that after a week of torrential rain, roads made of gooey - brown custard are not the best place for your first motorbike lesson!

ORINOCO FLOW.

If you fancy straying from the beaten track anywhere in Venezuela, just say "Humboldt". A couple of hundred years ago a complete nutter of that name ventured wherever westerners had previously been too scared or too sensible to go. In the Amazonas, "Ruta Humboldt" consists of a ten day journey that follows the Orinoco River deep into the jungle, before turning up some smaller tributaries and then (hopefully) rejoining the main river after a short overland trek.

Our own homage to Humboldt was to be made under the auspices of Oscar, a fluent guide and proud owner of a magnificently rounded belly, and the multi-talented Indian, Pepe, driver, machete-wielder and chef.

The ride to our departure point, Samariapo, was spent smearing ourselves with a mixture of baby lotion and mosquito repellent, designed to give the little bastards serious indigestion. Pepe, whose back was so pock-marked that it was virtually invisible under the bites, looked on with some amusement, while Oscar began his never-ending commentary, that was certainly fluent but sadly not in English.

Glistening like four prize-fighters, we slid into our little boat and were soon chugging along the Orinoco. To the right, the coffee and cocaine of Columbia, to the left, the relative safety of Venezuela, and beneath us, the unlikely combination of piranhas and pink dolphins.

My sensitive constitution proved no match for the combination of parasites and water-rat stew. As a consequence the first couple of days were spent performing a rather tedious ritual, standing knee deep in the river, shorts held aloof, with my rosy cheeks in full view of my companions, as pints of liquid dribbled between them. The only relief was that the rumours about Piranhas' penchant for human flesh proved unfounded!

Venturing further into the jungle we turned up the Casiquaire river, where we became increasingly enveloped by the green canopy of trees - a canopy that was only occasionally punctuated by the magnificent plumes of parrots. To add to the sense of claustrophobia, one of the engines packed in.

On day four we stumbled upon one of the local tribes, the Yanomami. Leaving Pepe downstream we presented ourselves, some machetes and some fishing hooks to the chief and were welcomed in. While the women wore jewellery (usually pieces of bone through their cheeks) most of the men were naked save for a small strip of red cloth. In her eagerness to catch this on film, one of my companions snapped once too often and we got to examine some impressive bows and arrows at close quarters, until the chief managed to intervene.

It soon emerged that dark-horse Oscar had fathered a child with one of the girls - girls being the right word since many of them have their first child immediately following puberty. We were invited to witness a traditional ceremony which in fact turned out to be a mass drug taking session. The make up of the powder, know as Yoppo, is a closely guarded secret, but its effectiveness was all too apparent.

All the men sat in a circle and took turns at letting one bloke blow drugs up his nose. As the Yoppo flew up each nostril in turn, each lucky recipient would grab the back of his head, as if holding his brains in, as blood started flying out of his nose. This delicate display was usually followed by vomiting.

The effects are strongly hallucinogenic, and the male who can handle the highest dose usually becomes chief. The Yanomami believe that Yoppo invokes spirits and so when someone has a bad trip it is the chief's responsibility to exorcise the evil.

It wasn't long before his services were required. One man began convulsing, his eyes rolling in fear. The chief knelt over him and leant forward. He then proceeded to sway to and fro, his hands coaxing the demons out of the prostrated figure. It was Oscar who stepped in for a hit (saving my own nasal passage from certain destruction) when the chief looked over expectantly in our direction.

It was at about this point that I became aware of a strange sound and ventured out to satisfy my curiosity. The women and children were all slapping themselves across the face, and emitting eerie guttural moans.

It transpired that one of the older women had died and that this was a mourning ritual that preceded burning the body and then eating the remains mixed with banana pulp. A bit more than I'd bargained for! Faster than you could say "Do you want ketchup on your dead person?" I was out of there. Although we were slightly delayed by Oscar who, along with all the other men, was tripping his tits off and was blissfully unaware of the tragedy.

Pepe was deeply unimpressed by our encounter with Yoppo, since to him it was tantamount to inviting demons into your life. By evening it looked as if he had a point for engine number two packed in, leaving us stranded in the middle of the river and soon after the mother of all storms broke out. The next five hours were spent huddled together under a small piece of tarpaulin, as torrential rain slowly filled the boat. All the while Pepe was trying to navigate a treacherous set of rapids in zero visibility.

After spending a lovely evening in this way, we awoke to discover that Oscar had come down with a fever and that even our resident action man could not fix the boat. Thankfully we had floated to a small settlement, where we borrowed a boat, and then set off for San Carlos de Rio Negro, the only place within a two hundred kilometres radius with an airstrip. It transpired that the airstrip would have had trouble qualifying as a muddy lane, and the aeroplane resembled a Skoda with armbands, but we jumped in gleefully! The Amazon? - Been there, not going back.!

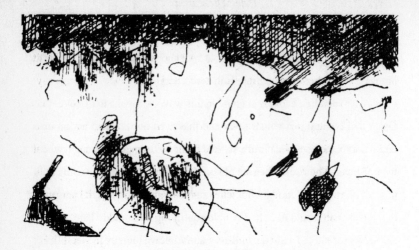

SPOOKSVILLE.

The scene before us was of the cloisters. Being only used to the plain conservatism of English cathedrals and cloisters, I was in awe and wonderment at the array of plants, trees, running water and fountains and above all geese, yes real live honking geese that were living within the cloisters. This living, moving, everyday scene was so far removed from my experience and expectations that all I could do was wander around, mouth wide open.

Eventually we came to the Cathedral door and followed the inevitable path inside. This time I wasn't so surprised. It was a Catholic shrine within an old building, and adorned with copious Baroque ornamentation attesting to the locals' history and faith. The choir was even older and more elaborate - a greater testament to its antiquity and Catholicism, but excessive for my minimalist needs. Nevertheless, we walked and observed and discussed and, like good tourists, took our photos. Suddenly I began to feel a little peculiar - I don't know how else to describe it. I was aware of a heavy, prickly sensation up the back of my head and behind my ears. It was becoming overpowering. I had to get out. I couldn't describe it in rational terms. I knew it was 'spooky', but not in the sense of ghosts or haunted houses. It didn't seem like a presence, a spiritual presence, and 'resonance' and 'energy' didn't seem quite right either.

I am writing this ten days after my first encounter, and the process alone is enough to evoke the creepiness. I still haven't come to any rational conclusions about the experience. Maybe I was here in a past life, but that doesn't sit very comfortably. Whatever it was/is, I do know that it happened, that it was real.

Was it heaven? Perhaps that's what the cloisters represented. I don't think it was hell. It might just be another dimension altogether.

THE SONGKHRAN CELEBRATIONS.

The road was closed to traffic and any parked vehicles were now hide-outs from behind which ambushes were being formed. I stood transfixed by the scampering figures, breathless from giggling, their drenched clothes sticking limply to their bodies. Then everything went black as a hand slimy with a mixture of water and prickly heat powder was rubbed over my face, and a couple of ice cubes slithered down my back!

We had arrived in Bangkok in mid April, coinciding with the height of the hot season and the Songkhran Festival, celebrating the Thai New Year. Songkhran, we had heard, was notable for the custom of throwing water over strangers in the street! It didn't promise to be the cultural high point of our trip so far!

All the usual stores selling T-shirts, watches and fake student cards had been cleared, and now served as military bases. They were stacked with multi-coloured weaponry which was being issued, at a price, by the usually inscrutable stall-holders. We made our way to the nearest, and selected a couple of 'Super Soakers', a '35 and a '58', ensuring that our price was high enough to guarantee refills from the tub of ammo by the side of the stall.

A six hour water fight ensued! As evening approached the battle died down. Everyone sat in the road to enjoy their grilled corn and plastic bags full of pineapple pieces and soft drinks. A sense of tranquillity settled over the street, of unity and quiet calm.

For the next two days, after the road was reopened, no-one was safe from the truck-loads of kids patrolling the streets. They beat drums and danced, curb-crawling passers-by and dousing them with water.

Then it was all over. The street stalls re-appeared and the kids went back to school. Travellers withdrew into their insular groups and spent their days lounging in cafes and watching videos, and the locals alternately ignored them or sold them things. Normality had resumed!

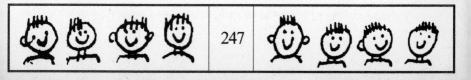

FLASH FLOOD.

The trek in the High Atlas mountains of Morocco proved to be an amazing and challenging experience. We explored green valleys, traversed mountain passes and climbed North Africa's highest mountain. We camped in sheltered valleys and on windy ridges, where the ground was so hard that the tent pegs bent and we had to weigh the tents with boulders to prevent them blowing away in the night. We washed in icy mountain streams, ate under the stars and marvelled at the tenacity of the Berbers, whose life style had hardly changed for centuries.

It was the penultimate day of our holiday and the most physically challenging. We'd hiked for hours in the mountains in temperatures reaching one hundred degrees farenheight, and I was exhausted but elated when we finally arrived at our campsite. We pitched our tents on a terrace about six feet above a stream, in a peaceful valley. Thankfully I removed my boots and crept into my sleeping bag to rest before supper.

As I lay in a semi-comatose state, fantasising about the hot shower and comfortable bed that awaited me on our return to Marrakech the next day, a violent storm arose. The thunder and lightening were accompanied by torrential rain and gale force winds which threatened to flatten our tent. Suddenly, we heard a long, low, rumbling noise, followed by frantic shouting in Arabic. My husband braved the deluge to discover the cause of alarm. He returned immediately, screaming at me to get up and run. Half asleep, I found myself being hauled from my sleeping bag and dragged across the terrace as a wall of water swept by. We were caught in a flash flood and had escaped death by less than six inches. We watched in horror as the once meandering stream was transformed into a raging torrent over one hundred yards wide and in which trees and boulders were propelled along at speeds of forty miles an hour.

Our tents and belongings were just above the water level, and as dusk descended we dragged and carried our equipment to higher ground. Within minutes, the campsite was flooded and I suddenly realised that I was soaked to the skin, my feet were cut and bleeding and I had started to shake from head to toe. We found refuge for the night in a Berber house, where the hospitable family took the arrival of twenty shocked, wet and dirty individuals in their stride. The following morning the whole extent of the tragedy became apparent. Entire villages and their occupants had been swept away, large sections of the road had disappeared and uprooted trees and huge boulders lay everywhere. We later discovered that a thousand people had perished.

I returned to England thankful to be alive and with lasting memories of the unselfishness, the heroism, the shared laughter and tears. One day, I will regale my grandchildren.

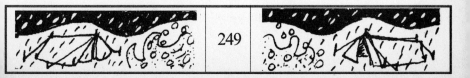

THE HOLY MAN.

"Strange things? What do you mean?"

"I cannot explain, madame, too difficult, but if you like to see, I take you there." The young Nepali winks and points to the cliff across the river.

The Bagmati is low, stagnant, the domain of fat grey monkeys squabbling over spoils from the temple. Toran takes my hand. Hopping on stepping stones is not easy with monkeys on your heels!

In the cave half-way up the cliff, the holy man has spotted us. A hasty blessing sends the Hindu pilgrims scuttling down the trail. They pass us, eyes down, and vanish through the trees.

The sun is hot, the path dusty and steep but Toran assures me I will never forget this holy man. "He does things, madame, no other man can do in the whole of Kathmandu." I struggle on and reach the cave in a sweat.

"Namaste." Our host leaps out of the shadows, a wild sort of a holy man, naked but for a loin cloth, with fierce rolling eyes and a mop of grey hair with a mind of its own.

"How much you pay?"

"Pay? I have no money..."

"Yesterday American lady pay ten dollars."

The man stares expectantly but I have nothing to offer. I prepare to leave.

"Wait..." I feel his gaze on my back, gripping like a metal hand. "For you, it is free."

The loin cloth lands at my feet. I glare at Toran.

"It is all right, madame. He will bear much pain but his mind is strong."

I hope so, for I can see where the pain will be. Our friend has gone into a trance, rubbing handfuls of dust between his legs.

The pliers came first, tinted with rust, prodding, squeezing, twisting his most manly parts into a knot of metal and flesh. The yogi squats, bounces on the spot, then slowly untangles himself with a satisfied moan.

"What is the point?" I whisper.

"This is warm up, madame. Now he will show you the real thing."

Real thing? My mind works overtime. A gust of wind whips up the dust and sends shivers trickling down my spine. The holy man takes no notice. Lost in meditation, he is smoothing his tender self back into shape. We wait respectfully. The minutes grow longer, the silence heavier.

"Relax, madame, no danger I promise." Toran tries to reassure, but his voice is uneasy. He knows what is coming and he is a shy man.

Suddenly our yogi is back on his feet, wide awake. "Here, you lift," he orders. I try but the rock barely moves. The man seems pleased.

"This way," he says, " for good view." I follow him into the light and sit on the step. The sun blazes down from a steel blue sky. The holy man squats on his haunches, grabs the end of his penis, pulls and pulls and hooks it under the rock. Am I dreaming, hypnotised? Surely this can't be, not that long, that strong... but as the man stands, the rock rises, balanced like magic.

"Take photo," groans the holy man, but I cannot. I am too busy watching! Toran has turned the other way. He is looking at the river and the monkeys below. But who is that? Another tourist coming up the trail?

The holy man does not complain. Business is good, and practice makes perfect!

CHINESE NIGHTLIFE.

Sailing out of Hong Kong harbour at night was an exciting and romantic experience. The brilliant neon Christmas lights of the skyscrapers gave way to the twinkling, ethereal night-lamps of passing river boats as we floated gently through the dark night towards Guangzhou. My lover and I embraced under the moonlight, excitedly anticipating the mystery and charm of China.

Romance evaporated quickly in our tiny cabin, when we discovered that our travelling companions were two wealthy, chain-smoking, Chinese insomniacs returning to Guangzhu with an enormous load of Christmas presents. After politely wishing us goodnight, they proceeded to try out each new computer game, toy and gadget, most of which played little tunes or emitted irritating electronic noises. If I ever have to spend another Christmas Eve listening to the squeaky voice of Minnie Mouse repeatedly wishing me a merry Christmas until 3 o'clock in the morning, I will personally take out a contract on the managing director of Walt Disney Enterprises!

I'm not sure how the stereotype of the silent, inscrutable Chinaman ever evolved. China was one of the noisiest places I have ever visited.

Our first three nights on dry land were spent in a building site. The owners called it a hotel, but in my opinion, a hotel is a place where you pay a lot of money to sleep, not to lie awake listening to the whine of drills and frenzied hammering. We soon discovered that nearly every hotel in China is currently being renovated, mostly after the guests had gone to bed.

A Buddhist monastery proved to be no escape. At four o'clock, the bedroom was shaken by a tremendous drum-roll, followed by the clash of cymbals and a blast of trumpets. The music, chanting, and prayers lasted an hour. At six o'clock they were repeated. At eight o'clock they were repeated and, ...

We returned to the secular world of half renovated hotels with dirty, draughty rooms, faulty wiring and dodgy lifts. But at least they didn't sing in the middle of the night!

Our trip was a bit like attending a month-long insomniacs conference. We had been looking for a relaxing quiet romantic time! Despite the fact it was very interesting, if I go again I'll take a big box of earplugs.

THE SOUND OF BULLETS.

Bullets don't sound the same as they do in the movies. They don't go "Pee-ow" when they ricochet. When machine bullets hit a wall, the noise is more like "Pink Pink Pink".

The people in Sayaxche's main street swarmed out of the shops and houses to see what the fuss was all about, only to scuttle back for cover when they realised that the attack was for real. Up in the first floor dining room, the Senora suggested for us to get out of sight of the road, under the table.

Apparently a group of guerrillas had come out of the jungle and shot up an army check point at the edge of town. Two soldiers had been killed before the rebels disappeared back into the bush. The Senora told us not to worry about the guerrillas. Though they occasionally killed soldiers, local people and tourists were usually safe. She didn't seem to know what they were fighting for. She said they could be leftist Indian peasants fighting the military regime, or perhaps a break-away army group. Like everyone else here in the remote Peten Province, she neither knew nor cared as long as it didn't affect her.

After the shootings, everything in town seemed to get back to normal very quickly. It wasn't as if anything particularly out of the ordinary had happened. The canoe-powered raft that served as a ferry still plied the river whenever there were vehicles for it to take across and the town had resumed the sleepy air that it had when we had first arrived. Apart from the ever-present soldiers, there was no sign of any hostilities. We crossed the river and boarded the afternoon bus for the nearby town of Flores, a journey which, apart from the usual army searches, was uneventful until we finally arrived and were just getting off the bus.

We had barely set foot in the street when the air seemed to explode around us. A staccato noise like hundreds of small thunder claps, clattered off in rapid succession and out of the corner of my eye I could see smoke and orange flashes. Our next move was instinctive. We dived for the cover of the nearest wall and threw ourselves onto the ground. Half expecting the next burst to be aimed our way, I glanced up, trying to work out where the bullets were coming from, but all I could see were the feet of the other passengers who were calmly carrying on getting off the bus. A few stopped and stared at us. Then they walked off to join their friends who were setting off fire crackers at the fiesta that was just starting in the plaza across the street.

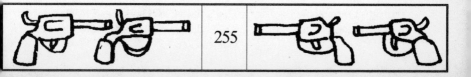

The 'Travellers' Tales From Heaven & Hell' competition will continue to be run annually, so why not send us your own entry in under 500 words. Each year we have some fantastic prizes on offer such as flights to anywhere in the world, weekend breaks, travel guides etc.

TravellersEye Club Membership

Each month we receive hundreds of enquiries from people who've read our books or entered our competitions. All of these people have one thing in common: an aching to achieve something extraordinary, outside the bounds of our everyday lives. Not everyone can undertake the more extreme challenges, but we all value learning about other people's experiences.

Membership is free because we want to unite people of similar interests. Via our website, members will be able to liase with each other about everything from the kit they've taken, to the places they've been to and the things they've done. Our authors will also be available to answer any of your questions if you're planning a trip or if you simply have a question about their books.

As well as regularly up-dating members with news about our forthcoming titles, we will also offer you the following benefits:

Free entry to author talks / signings
Direct author correspondence
Discounts off new & past titles
Free entry to TravellersEye events
Discounts on a variety of travel products & services

To register your membership, simply write or e-mail us at the address given in the front of the book, telling us your details.

Others titles currently available from TravellersEye:

More Travellers' Tales From Heaven & Hell	ISBN: 1903070023	£6.99
Touching Tibet	ISBN: 0953057550	£7.99
Fever Trees Of Borneo	ISBN: 0953057569	£7.99
The Jungle Beat	ISBN: 0953057577	£7.99
Discovery Road	ISBN: 0953057534	£7.99
Frigid Women	ISBN: 0953057526	£7.99
Trail Of Visions, Route 1	ISBN: 1871349338	£14.99
Trail Of Visions, Route 2	ISBN 095305750X	£16.99